P9-EJH-329

*Twayne's English Authors Series*

*Sylvia E. Bowman, Editor*

INDIANA UNIVERSITY

*Ada Leverson*

152

# Ada Leverson

By CHARLES BURKHART
*Temple University*

Twayne Publishers, Inc. : : New York

Library of Congress Catalog Card Number: 72-13370



ISBN 0-8057-1330-1
MANUFACTURED IN THE UNITED STATES OF AMERICA

*For*
*Violet Wyndham*

# *Preface*

THE revival of interest in Ada Leverson, which began with the republication of her six novels by Chapman and Hall in 1950 and 1951, may have been one origin of the revival of interest in everything Edwardian, an interest which is still lively today, as in the present fad for *art nouveau.* No one is more of the 1890's and the Edwardian period than Mrs. Leverson, in one sense; but, because her talent lay in comedy and satire, with all that they imply of judgment and objectivity, no other novelist of the period could be said, in another and more important sense, to be more apart from her age. Unlike those Realists or Naturalists of the era who recorded the end of the Victorian age with a grim pessimism or an idealistic revolt, she opted for the comic spirit. To define the nature of her comedy, I have discussed the kinds of comedy popular in the 1890's with readers and audiences and how her writing embodies them; for the same reason, I have compared her with other leading comic writers at the turn of the century like Oscar Wilde and H. H. Munro ("Saki"). If Wilde is the master of comedy of manners in this period, she is the mistress. Her comedy of manners differs from his in that it is not heartless. Her characters are allowed, in a way that his are not, the impulse of passion and the softness of sentiment.

Her earliest pieces were written for publications of the 1890's like *Punch* and the *Yellow Book;* her friendship with Wilde lasted from 1892 to his death in 1900; she was, at that same period, a hostess celebrated for her wit and her high style. The 1890's were formative years for her both as woman and as writer; therefore, I have devoted one chapter to a brief biography of Mrs. Leverson which shows how the events of her life, particularly from the time of her marriage until the death of Wilde, conditioned her outlook, and provided her with her chief theme—marriage. Her writings are like her, that is, they directly concern her life, so that here, if ever, a biographical approach to literary criticism can be justified; but it should be added that there is always, because of her reserve, breeding, and comic detachment, a certain distancing to the life experiences that eventually take shape in her fiction. Her life has been written by her daughter, Violet Wyndham, in *The Sphinx and Her Circle*, a book which will often be referred to; the present book is the first full-length critical study of Ada Leverson's writings.

Another chapter in the present book, one which follows the biographical chapter, is called "Ada Leverson's London"; it comments upon the historical role of setting in literature, and it then attempts to show with what powers of observation Mrs. Leverson saw Mayfair in the years in which her six novels were published, 1907 to 1916, and to record numerous examples of her lively attention to the surface of life in that period. One of the great interests that fiction supplies is a sense of the past: it gives us not just the manners and morals of the past but what things looked like then —buildings, clothing, streets, shops. Thus, faithful recorders like James Joyce have shown us Dublin, or Marcel Proust has shown us Paris, or Mrs. Leverson has shown us London. Today certain places in England have become national literary shrines—Stratford, the Lake Country, Haworth in Yorkshire; what survives in, and what has changed from, the records that William Shakespeare, William Wordsworth, and the Brontë sisters Emily and Charlotte have left of those places is probably what interests their visitors most—how history persists and how it is altered. Mrs. Leverson's London is not so ranging and rich a picture as Charles Dickens' London, yet her smaller canvas is almost as crowded as his, and her critics from the beginning have commented upon her meticulous evocations of the details and the spirit of the setting she chose for her novels. The same interest is also found in the essays, sketches, parodies, short stories, and weekly columns she wrote. Two chapters deal with these shorter pieces, which have not been fully or systematically described before.

Since Mrs. Leverson is a minor novelist and since she chose to cover small canvases rather than large ones, her works lend themselves to a consideration of the esthetics of fiction. Major novelists are revolutionaries; minor novelists are more easily seen within a tradition and more fruitfully compared to their contemporaries. However, Mrs. Leverson's novels have been approached at least as much for their own interest and value as for the formal considerations of the genre that they suggest. She was the least portentous of writers, though a very serious one; she was too civilized a writer and a woman for an obtrusive apparatus of critical theory to be appropriately applied. We can no more than try to imitate the quick insights, the deep questions behind the gaiety, and the sensitive alertness to the false and ridiculous, as well as to the elegant and the good.

CHARLES BURKHART

*Temple University*

# *Acknowledgments*

THIS book was made possible by the generous access to family papers granted to me by Violet Wyndham, the daughter of Ada Leverson. And, in many other ways, by thoughtful suggestion and careful criticism, Mrs. Wyndham was liberality itself.

I am also deeply grateful for the assistance I received from Sir Rupert Hart-Davis; from Mrs. Eva G. Reichmann; from the late Herman Schrijver, Esq.; from the late Professor W. K. Rose; from Mr. Joe C. Rees, of the Duke University Library, whose bibliographical expertise helped me in this and earlier books; and from Temple University, which materially aided me in my research and writing.

For permission to quote from published works, I wish to thank Violet Wyndham, for her own and her mother's works; J-P R. Ross, Esq., for letters from Ada Leverson to Alec Ross; Chapman and Hall, for Mrs. Leverson's novels; W. W. Norton, for *The Little Ottleys;* Vanguard, for *The Sphinx and Her Circle;* Duckworth, for *Letters to the Sphinx from Oscar Wilde;* Sir Rupert Hart-Davis, for *The Letters of Oscar Wilde;* Little, Brown, for Sir Osbert Sitwell's *Noble Essences;* Macmillan, for Sir William Rothenstein's *Since Fifty: Men and Memories 1922–1938;* Methuen, for Harold Acton's *Memoirs of an Aesthete.*

# *Contents*

# *Chronology*

1862 Ada Esther Beddington born, London, October 10.
1881 Married Ernest Leverson.
1892 Met Oscar Wilde.
1892 Began to write stories, parodies, sketches, and series of letters for *Black and White* and *Punch.*
1895 Wilde arrested. Sheltered by Leversons between trials. Wilde imprisoned.
1895 First story, "Suggestion," in *Yellow Book.*
1896 Second story, "The Quest of Sorrow," in *Yellow Book.*
1897 Wilde released from prison.
1897 Last sketch appeared in *Punch.*
1900 Death of Oscar Wilde.
1903 Began weekly column for *Referee.*
1905 Ended weekly column for *Referee.*
1907 *The Twelfth Hour.*
1908 *Love's Shadow.*
1911 *The Limit.*
1912 *Tenterhooks.*
1914 *Bird of Paradise.*
1916 *Love at Second Sight.*
1919 First of three sketches in *English Review.*
1922 Death of Ernest Leverson.
1926 Memoir of Wilde, "The Last First Night," published in *Criterion.*
1930 *Letters to the Sphinx from Oscar Wilde.*
1933 Died, London, August 30, aged seventy.

# CHAPTER 1

## *Ada Leverson's Life*

THE story of Ada Leverson's life has been told with such authority by Violet Wyndham in *The Sphinx and Her Circle: A Memoir of Ada Leverson by Her Daughter*[1] that any later account, whether biographical or critical, must first acknowledge its indebtedness to Mrs. Wyndham's book. The easy candor and grace of the memoir are reminiscent of the Sphinx herself, and thus her daughter's book has the double authority of firsthand knowledge and of the power of evocation. Much, indeed most, of what is about to be recounted of Ada Leverson's life inevitably derives from *The Sphinx and Her Circle;* what will be emphasized here, however, is her literary life, although it will soon enough be seen that there is little distinction between Mrs. Leverson as writer and as woman.

The same point could be made of Mrs. Gaskell or of Charlotte Brontë, but not, I think, of Virginia Woolf or of Katherine Mansfield. In other words, some writers do not adopt a persona in their work to the extent that other writers do. They feel less need of masks, and the result for the reader is a certain sense of directness and integrity in the vision he is encountering. Virginia Woolf's artifice can be subtle or it can be obtrusive: in either case, her work stands between us and her. Mrs. Leverson's novels are not, of course, direct transcripts of her life—no novels ever are. But the particular candor just mentioned as characteristic of her daughter's work informs her own; therefore, an account of her life is a useful introduction to a study of her work.

### I *Family and Marriage*

She was born Ada Esther Beddington on October 10, 1862, at 21 Hyde Park Square in London. Her paternal grandfather was a highly successful wool merchant; her maternal grandfather was

Sir John Simon, M.P. for Dewbury for twenty years. The maternal ancestry was marked by a strongly liberal and intellectual tradition. One ancestor, Don Cesar Orobio, was a Marrano Jew of Braganza who was burned at the stake in the 1600's for refusing to renounce his faith. His son left Spain for the French court and became physician to Louis XIV; but, because the open practice of the Jewish religion was forbidden in France, he once again migrated, this time to Amsterdam, where, as an eminent scholar and a friend of Baruch Spinoza, he lived out the rest of his life. A still later descendant, Isaac Simon, led the cause of emancipation in Jamaica; and he is said to have been the first owner to liberate his slaves. It is not farfetched to see an echo of family history in Ada Leverson's own liberality of outlook, in principles of kindness and generosity which almost seem to be ingrained.[2]

When Ada's mother, née Zillah Simon, was painted by John Everett Millais, he portrayed an elegant woman whose fine eyes and alert smile reveal both poise and temperament. Her chief interest was music, and she was a highly accomplished pianist. Her daughter Ada inherited the taste for music (as is shown by the frequent references to operas and concerts and musicians in her writing), but not the talent in performance.

There are also eccentric gentlemen, both young and old, in the novels, and Ada's father, Samuel Henry Beddington, seems, from his granddaughter's description, to have had a hypochondriac oddity or two. For example, "he ate only roast chicken, fried sole, boiled salmon, or apple tart, and drank only white wine, barley water, or tea."[3] In the mansion in Hyde Park Square the four sons and four daughters born to Zillah and Samuel grew up, despite the occasionally autocratic behavior of their father, in an atmosphere of cultured ease and prosperity that was conducive to self-development and self-expression—a setting that we associate with late Victorian culture at its best.

Ada, the eldest daughter, showed an early aptitude for letters, and her father engaged a classics tutor for her. Throughout her life she read constantly; and like her, the heroines of her novels are frequently portrayed as reading and discussing books. But she was not a bluestocking, any more than her heroines are. She was always gladly social, and, as a debutante, she attended dances and engaged in the round of activities open to a young unmarried woman of her class.

Her three sisters made brilliant marriages. The first husband of Evelyn, Ada's next younger sister, died young; her second husband was Walter Behrens, president of the Chamber of Commerce in Paris. The next sister, Sybil, whom a drawing by Paul-César Helleu shows as a spirited and elegant young woman, married David Seligman; but the chief romantic interest in her life for many years was the composer Giacomo Puccini. The youngest of the Beddington girls, Violet, married Sydney Schiff, better known as the writer Stephen Hudson, whose major work, still unappreciated, is *A True Story* (1930). *A True Story* is a Proustian, Joycean, and autobiographical compilation of three of his earlier novels, *Richard Kurt, Prince Hempseed,* and *Elinor Colhouse.*[4]

Ada was nineteen when Ernest Leverson, thirty-one, the son of a rich diamond merchant, proposed to her; and she accepted him immediately. Her ready acceptance reminds us of one of her famous jokes, this one in a letter many years later to Harold Acton, who was staying at the seaside in Hastings: that "to marry at Hastings would be to repent at St. Leonard's."[5] She married Ernest against her father's wishes—to free herself from just such displays of parental authority; but she also made her decision because she was susceptible to the glamour of a man considerably older than she and altogether more experienced.

Their basic incompatibility was soon revealed. Ernest's greater experience became less attractive when it was discovered to include the fathering of an illegitimate daughter who was being reared in a convent in Paris. At first there may have been an attraction of opposites between Ada and Ernest, but, when his two chief interests, gambling and horses, became the realities of daily married life, the attraction faded. She could not share these interests, nor does it seem likely that he could more than superficially appreciate her wit, her character, her charm. The one similarity between them was a huge hazard from the beginning and in the end proved the downfall of their marriage: neither had a strong business sense. Or, rather, Ernest had a bad business sense; Ada, none at all.

Still, the surface of their life in the 1880's was agreeable, and their extravagance helped make it appear so. They lived at No. 2 Courtfield Gardens in South Kensington which, in those days, was a more fashionable district than it later became; Ada had her dresses from Paquin, Ernest his journeys to Paris and Monte Carlo; they had a son and a daughter; they entertained, and they frequented good society. The long-suffering heroine of three of Mrs. Leverson's novels, Edith Ottley, gives a clue as to how the marriage survived as long as it did. Bruce, Edith's husband, is extravagant, a petty tyrant, a flirt, and much more; but Edith, through cleverness, tact, and good humor, manages him, the children, and the household. She will not divorce him any more than Mrs. Leverson would divorce her husband, for divorce was scandalous, public, and demeaning.

Like Edith in her love for Aylmer Ross, Mrs. Leverson had her romantic attachments: with William, the fourth Earl of Desart, a handsome young Irish poet; with Prince Henri d'Orléans, the explorer and writer; with George Moore, who had returned from his years in Paris and was attempting to take literary London by storm.[6] Throughout her life, Ada, like her heroine Edith Ottley, preferred the company of men to that of women. Already in the 1880's she seems to have known most people of consequence in the art and literary worlds of London. Her drawing room was as near a salon as the English achieve. She was already becoming celebrated for her wit. The stuffier members of her husband's family and of her own disapproved of the freedom and fashion of her life; perhaps they envied its glitter.

The portraits and photographs of her that survive show her style and her breeding and that strange enigmatic expression which makes "the Sphinx," the name Oscar Wilde gave her, so apt. Neither quite a smile, nor a frown, the expression is a certain fixity of regard which makes the pictured face both intimate and remote, both meaningful and ambiguous. It is candid, but with a suggestion of depths; above all, it is highly intelligent. The face is neither beautiful nor plain, but it is arresting. What there is of beauty is the golden hair,—which made her Wilde's "gilded" Sphinx; the pallor of her skin; the jade-green eyes.

With her looks, her position, her wit, what was it that led her to begin to write? She was thirty when her first story was published. It is very clear—there is abundant testimony—that it was not the desire for fame or money. It may have been that she sought some stronger expression of herself than the impermanence of conversation gave; it may have been that brilliant society and the success with which she kept an impossible marriage possible were not, finally, enough; or it may have been that whatever makes a person an artist, the basic subconscious creative urge, had taken this while to form itself and to force its way into the light. Whatever the cause, the catalyst was probably Oscar Wilde.

## II *Oscar Wilde*

In the end, Wilde seems to have turned against everyone, or at least to have subjugated everyone to despotic temporary banishment, which made the eventual reconciliation with him all the more painful and theatrical. Lacerated beyond endurance by his fall, he made the ignominy of his final years splendid, a kind of royalty of sordidness. This is the impression which his letters, his best literature outside the one perfect play, seem to suggest. He was essentially literary, fatally so; he tried to shape his life in the way unreal lives are shaped in fiction—and the raw, crude flux of the real overwhelmed that narrow, intense effort.

But to one friend, Ada Leverson, he remained exquisite, and to her he was the one great event of her life, to which the early years led up and the later years returned. Ada Leverson met Oscar Wilde in 1892, at a party given by Mrs. Oswald Crawfurd,[7] when Ada was thirty and he was thirty-eight. It was not long before he was calling her "the wittiest woman in the world." His friendship for her survived even his later quarrels with Ernest, because it was a friendship founded on their mutual love for comedy, elegance, and affectation. She herself was not affected but playfully urged others to be,[8] and some of his letters or frequent telegrams to her—she once said that she planned to edit "The Collected Telegrams of Oscar Wilde"—must have gratified this desire: "You are one of those—alas, too few—who are always followed by the flutes of the pagan world." Or: "I shall be in town soon, and must come and charm the Sphinx with honey-cakes. The trouble is I left my flute in a railway carriage—and the fauns take so long to cut new reeds."[9]

Even though the friendship formed in 1892 lasted uninterruptedly until Wilde's death in 1900, Mrs. Leverson's early admiration of Wilde often took the form of parody when, inspired by Wilde's triumphs and by his urging, she began to contribute stories and sketches to *Black and White* and to *Punch*. Parody is an ambiguously sincere form of flattery; however, the four sketches that appeared in *Punch* from 1893 to 1895 (discussed in more detail in Chapter 3) are cool, harmless, funny skits—on *The Picture of Dorian Gray, The Sphinx, An Ideal Husband,* and *The Importance of Being Earnest.* The second of these parodies, "The Minx—A Poem in Prose," caused Wilde to begin to call her his "Sphinx." His poem *The Sphinx* is a long Baudelairean erotic fantasy which was first published in 1894 in an elaborate format with decorations by Charles Ricketts. Mrs. Leverson's *Punch* parody was illustrated by Edward Tennyson Reed with a caricature of Ricketts' design for the cover of *The Sphinx.*[10]

In the same year appeared Robert Hichens' *The Green Carnation;* Wilde at first suspected Mrs. Leverson of its authorship. In it Wilde is caricatured as Esmé Amarinth and Douglas as Lord Reginald Hastings. As a *succès de scandale,* it is long forgotten; as a book, it is a particular kind of failure which results, I think, from a confusion in authorial intention: it proceeds from divided aims—to satirize Wilde and to render him ridiculous but, at the same time, seriously to analyze Wilde's life-esthetic and, to carry it even further, to out-paradox Wilde—if such a word is possible, and if such an aim is credible. Thus, *The Green Carnation* is sharply comic in some places; in others, it quite seriously explores the implications of "art for art's sake." At times, the novel sounds more like Wilde than Wilde does; at others, the caricature is coarse. The success of the book added to Wilde's growing notoriety; it is suggestive just on the discreet side of libel; it would be highly interesting to know what Mrs. Leverson herself thought of the book, sinces Wilde thought it both clever and vulgar.[11] It is not conceivable, however, that so evasive a mélange could have come from the purely lucid and straightforward pen of Mrs. Leverson.

Mrs. Leverson became friendly with Wilde's intimates—Lord Alfred Douglas, Robert Ross, Reggie Turner, and others—and dined with them often at Willis's in King Street, St. James's, the most fashionable restaurant of the 1890's.[12] We wonder what attitude Ernest Leverson took toward his wife's ever widening circle of friends; undoubtedly he was tolerant, not indifferent, because he himself not only was friendly with Wilde and Douglas but later showed great kindness to Wilde.

For Wilde's last great premiere, *The Importance of Being Earnest* on February 14, 1895, Wilde gave the Sphinx a box to which she invited Aubrey and Mabel Beardsley; the enormous success of that night was the height of his career; by sinister but inevitable conjunction, it was on that same night that the Marquess of Queensberry, Lord Alfred's father, left Wilde the bouquet of vegetables at the theater from which he was barred; and Wilde's downfall had begun.

The climax of the relationship of the Leversons and Oscar Wilde has been narrated so often that when the name Ada Leverson is recognized by someone unfamiliar with her novels, the invariable reaction is, "Yes, the woman who sheltered Wilde during his trials." The story has been told best by Mrs. Leverson herself in a small limited-edition book of 1930, her last published work, now very rare and costly: *Letters to the Sphinx from Oscar Wilde, with Reminiscences of the Author.*[13] The thirty letters themselves, we are told by Sir Rupert Hart-Davis in his edition of Wilde's letters, are "heavily cut and doctored";[14] but the essay on Wilde which prefaces them[15] is the authentic evocation of Wilde and the most vivid account we have, outside his own letters, of what he was like at that desperate period. No hotel would admit him, and he accepted the Leversons' offer of the nursery rooms on an upper floor. He passed his days among hobbyhorses and golliwogs, and he descended to the drawing room each evening for several hours, where he talked as well as he ever had—and contemporary testimony agrees that he was the greatest talker of his day.

In a sense, it was a more surprising act of charity to offer Wilde a resting place on Ernest Leverson's part than on his wife's, since, despite his generally liberal outlook, he was in some ways a conventional City gentleman. In fact, he behaved with perfect magnanimity to Wilde through his trial and his two years of imprisonment, lending him a large sum of money, helping to manage his business affairs, and buying in a bankruptcy sale several of Wilde's paintings for him. Wilde repaid him at first with sincere gratitude but later, after prison had weakened and warped him, with the harsh and quite unfounded accusation that Leverson had withheld his (Wilde's) money.[16]

To the Sphinx no cloud of suspicion could ever be attached in Wilde's mind. With other friends, she met him on his release from prison; she visited him in Paris in 1898 and was faithfully devoted to him until his death two years later. Perhaps the nearly unique steadfastness of Wilde's regard for her was his recognition of her essential openheartedness. It was impossible for him to be other than gentle with her. Her own malice was so sunny that it seldom provoked retaliation; he could not let himself doubt her, even though he eventually doubted most of the world, including himself.

## III *Early Prose and Life*

The four parodies of Wilde already referred to, together with the story of her friendship for Wilde, illustrate the closeness of Ada Leverson's life to her art. Critical accounts of her writings are given in later chapters; but, since her writings are inseparable from the events of her biography, they need mention here. People she knew, experiences she had had, and jokes and stories she had heard or originated appear sometimes with little transformation in her stories and novels.

The earliest works by her that I know of are three short stories and a series of "Letters of Silvia and Aurelia," all of which appeared in the weekly journal *Black and White* from 1892 to 1894. A more suitable outlet for her talents was found in *Punch*, for which she began to write in July, 1893. The verve and sophistication of *Punch* suited her own bent; she contributed parodies of Max Beerbohm, George Moore, and others, along with the Wilde parodies, as well as several series of letters—"Letters to [or from] a Debutante," "Letters to [or from] a Fiancée," and "Letters of Marjorie and Gladys"—and various miscellaneous pieces. These works reflect her own social life and London life in general. She continued to write for *Punch* until 1897.[17]

Her closeness to the art movements of the 1890's is shown by a request that she contribute to the *Yellow Book*, the central art and literary periodical of the time, whose other contributors ranged from Max Beerbohm to Aubrey Beardsley to George Moore. For this brief but important journal she wrote two stories. Her association with the *Yellow Book* recalls her future publisher Grant Richards' remark that she was "the Egeria of the whole Nineties movement."[18]

Even geographically she became central. It was still the day of horse-drawn carriages: feeling that South Kensington lay too far from the center of things, she and her family moved to Mayfair and into a small Regency house, No. 4 Deanery Street, off Park Lane and opposite Stanhope Gate. She was happy in the bustle of the heart of London; she loved London with a passion, and her novels are as urban as any ever written. The move to Deanery Street in 1896 also offered some compensation for the death of her son and the increasing deterioration of her marriage. The repression of her private sorrows must have contributed to the public image of Sphinx-like sophisticate. Her airy gaieties were her intrinsic self, not a mere mask; but another part of herself was a capacity for suffering—one which, with admirable decorum, she let few of her associates ever catch a glimpse of.

Next, in 1903, she undertook a regular column for the *Referee,* a weekly of the popular type. Perhaps her entry into this sort of journalism was compelled by the worsening financial position of Ernest. In any case the task was arduous; under the pen name of "Elaine" she wrote a hundred and thirteen of her "White and Gold" columns from 1903 to 1905. Such unremitting labor may have caused her to turn to the more spacious effort required in writing novels; or the publisher Grant Richards may at last have been successful in his persuasions;[19] or the end of her own marriage may have led to her wish to write of marriage: the central theme of her novels. Her own union ended in separation, not divorce, when Ernest, who had lost most of his money in the City, and who was accompanied by his illegitimate daughter, emigrated to Canada where he lived until his death in 1922. As a result of Ernest's defection and losses, the pretty house in Deanery Street had to be exchanged for a house in Radnor Place, Hyde Park, near enough to her father's house in Hyde Park Square that his secretary-housekeeper, Miss Hudson, could manage the practical affairs of the household which Mrs. Leverson by temperament and training was incapable of conducting.[20]

She did not become a novelist until the age of forty-five. The novels ceased—it seems abruptly, since almost all novelists, once they start, do not stop—nine years later; but there is nothing middle-aged about the six books from *The Twelfth Hour* (1907) to *Love at Second Sight* (1916). Immersed in the art and literature of the day, a close friend to many young painters and writers, and a *mondaine* in the best sense, she was as fresh an observer of life as she had been when she left her father's house at the age of nineteen, and as she was to be to the end of her days. A sense of comedy can help to keep one young and, from the testimony of her daughter and her friends, her latter years were bright ones.

The tragedies of her life were over, and her novels were well received and widely read. If unhappiness had caused her to begin writing them, happiness—or, if that is too strong a word, a lively contentment—may have caused her to stop. An artist in creating the balanced world of his painting or his poem is compensating for some imbalance within himself—some wound, some frustration, some overwhelming question. If this concept is too Freudian and schematic an explanation of why Mrs. Leverson ceased to write novels, and if it makes the failure of her marriage too central and operative in her inspiration, we can simply say that she knew how to live even better than she knew how to write. Once financially secure, she, relying on the love and generosity of her daughter, abandoned herself gaily to life. It would be easy to say that World War I darkened her outlook, and, in fact, the war is important to her last novel; but there is no evidence that her outlook darkened—what evidence there is, is to the contrary. We miss the novels she might have written had she continued, but not even a literary critic could begrudge her the joys of her later life—her travel, her family, a first night of the Russian Ballet, or a first performance of *Façade*.

## IV *Later Life, Friends, and Publications*

In her later years, when people began to think back on the 1890's, now remote enough to be viewed objectively, and after Wilde's literary reputation had been resuscitated and the Sphinx's role in his life and in the entire decade of the 1890's movement remembered, Mrs. Leverson became something of a legend. We catch glimpses of her in biographies, memoirs, and editions of letters, momentary appearances in which she wears the aura of earlier events, awakens echoes of an earlier age. A typical example is the following passage from Sir William Rothenstein's memoirs of the year 1930: "I wanted to take Oliver Lodge and my wife to I Tatti, the Berensons' villa at Settignano, but the Berensons were travelling in Greece, the villa was closed, so we could not see the treasures there. Happily, Reginald Turner, most genial of men and wittiest of talkers, whom I saw all too rarely, was in Florence. There, too, I met for the last time Ada Leverson, Oscar Wilde's 'Sphinx,' a strange figure from the past, now grown old, but gay and vivacious still."[21]

After World War I, Ada had moved from the house in Radnor Place to a flat at No. 60 South Audley Street; in her final years, she lived at the Washington Hotel in Curzon Street. Thus she was back in Mayfair, the part of London she liked best. A *pied-à-terre* in a congenial hotel made it easier for her to travel, and in the 1920's she spent part of most winters in Florence. She was evidently a good traveler; she liked motor cars, the faster the better; she appeared in Amalfi or on the Côte d'Azur, often accompanying the Sitwells.

Osbert Sitwell enacted nearly the same role for her that Wilde had earlier played. Her devotion to him, as well as to Edith and Sacheverell, was one of the centers of her life. She praised their work to any who would listen; she introduced them to writers and artists of her own age, like Max Beerbohm; and through them she in turn met the gifted young. There were friends from the past, like Reginald Turner; but also there were always new friends. Although her circle was smaller than in the 1890's, to recite the names that comprised it is almost like hearing a roll call of the English literary scene. In addition to those already mentioned, her friends included Harold Acton, Peter Quennell, Ronald Firbank, and many more.

Reggie Turner, one of Wilde's closest friends, was an unsuccessful novelist but a successful expatriate in Florence. His biographer, Stanley Weintraub, believes that the character Ida Courtney in Turner's novel *Samson Unshorn* is "an Ada Leverson type"; but the details fit Mrs. Julia Frankau, who wrote under the name of "Frank Danby," much more closely than they do the Sphinx.[22] As for Harold Acton's mention of Mrs. Leverson in his *Memoirs of an Aesthete*, it could not be called uniformly kind, since Acton makes Ada's fondness for the Sitwells border on obsession, and he pictures her as slightly grotesque, though he noticed, as Wilde had a generation earlier, her resemblance to Sarah Bernhardt. But the farewell to her in the last pages of his book is gentler:

> The Sphinx was no more, and one would never again be entertained in the same unexpected, disconnected way, by her preposterous puns about Serge Figleafer and Lords Rathermore and Beavercrook, by the chuckling insight and inner hearing under her apparent deafness, which she could open and shut like a snuff-box, distributing sneezes

of laughter, by her memories of the legendary Oscar Wilde, so alive to herself and to Reggie. The last time I had seen her she told me a latterday anecdote about Oscar in Paris. He had romanced to her somewhat fulsomely about a beautiful young *apache,* who was so attached to Oscar that he always accompanied him with a knife in one hand. "I'm sure he had a fork in the other," said the Sphinx. I had left her chuckling to herself in the dim lounge of a frigid hotel. . . . It was comforting to know that she had died in a good humour, having bequeathed her worldly goods and chattels and musical instruments, purely imaginary, to Osbert Sitwell.[23]

The longest account of Mrs. Leverson in this period of her life is the chapter Sir Osbert Sitwell devotes to her in his autobiographical volume *Noble Essences.* It does not concern her writing; rather, it is a *portrait souvenir* of the Sphinx as companion, wit, friend, and protector of Wilde. The account is not always accurate; for a niggling example, the date of her death is given as 1936—an error in which many a later critic or reviewer has followed him—though Sir Osbert himself wrote the obituary which appeared in the *Times* on September 1, 1933. Despite the insight and richness of anecdote in Sir Osbert's chapter, the tone is a little patronizing; his style, we might add, in its elaboration and preciosity strikes us as much more dated than Ada Leverson's clear, quick prose. I simply cannot believe that Mrs. Leverson was in the habit of "invariably" welcoming a visitor to her flat by pouring an entire bottle of scent over him—"always Chanel, *Numéro Cinq.*"[24] But other of Sir Osbert's anecdotes and glimpses have the stamp of authenticity, and we are grateful for their vividness and sympathy:

As a rule, when I, or any other friend of hers, went to see her of an afternoon in the hotel in London in which she usually made her home in the summer, we would be sure to find her in the corner of a vast public room, a little figure in black, sitting on a large sofa, a black satin bag and a paper-bound French book by her side, quite alone, but shaking with irrepressible laughter. This laughter was at many things, at incidents which had occurred, and at incidents which had not occurred, at things people had said or that, in fact, they had not said, but which had been suggested to her by the marriage of her deafness to her wit. On one afternoon, I remember, she was laughing at the memory of a party the evening before: what desperation the guests have been suffering within themselves that would have been sufficient to make them abandon their homes, and drive them out thus, on the blackest and coldest night of the year, to a gathering of which they could entertain so few, and yet such deceptive, hopes?[25]

And this glimpse of her and Ronald Firbank—what a conjunction of comic spirits!—in Florence is presented by Sir Osbert: "Occasionally he could be seen in her hotel, peeping in a rather disconsolate and helpless manner over the top of an enormous bouquet he had bought on his way here to present to her. . . ."[26] Of her first meeting with Arthur Waley, at a tea party given by Edith Sitwell, Sir Osbert records that Arthur "took a seat by her side, but remained silent, thinking of other things, when Sphinx, who was in a mischievous mood that afternoon, broke the ice by turning to him and saying suddenly: 'I suppose *you* often go to *The Mikado,* Mr. Waley?' "[27] And we find also this memorable description of Mrs. Leverson in Amalfi:

She grew to love Italy—although it is true that she knew it only within the limited orbit of a sunny terrace or two, and of a few streets. In particular she liked the hotel at Amalfi, with its garden and stupendous view. There below, in the town from which the servants were drawn, life remained old-fashioned, with the primitive poverty of the houses of peasants and fishermen of which the place was composed, so that, to those who tended and looked after her, she must have seemed a very artful and artificial being. What can they have understood, one party of the other? For example, several of the peasant servants could not read—and Sphinx's life was consumed in reading: they spoke no English, she no Italian. But it was quickly evident that she had won their affection, and in spite of their natural southern indolence, and their inquisitiveness—which made them want to stop to talk to everyone they met on the way—they would hurry on her errands. She never walked far, but towards the evening she could often be seen trailing her cloak in the sunset, tasting the cool fragrance of the Neapolitan dusk, scented with lemon blossom and roses. Sometimes she would pause and look up longingly over her head at a tangerine, just out of reach of her grasp—rather as if, in the manner of the fabulous marauding seal or *vacca marina,* which was believed locally to dwell in a cavern below the cliffs and to come out at nightfall to scale and rob the orange trees of their precious load, she intended to climb and snatch at the fruit, for which, though her appetite was always so small, she had formed a great liking.[28]

Sir Osbert also describes Ada's first meeting with Henry James:

> On the first occasion she had sat next Henry James at dinner, she had not been able to resist putting to him certain questions about his books, for she had been a lifelong admirer of them, and . . . at last, after he had answered some of these murmured inquiries, he had turned his melancholy gaze upon her, and had said to her, "Can it be—it must be—that you are the embodiment of the incorporeal, that elusive yet ineluctable being to whom through the generations novelists have so unavailingly made invocation; in short, the *Gentle Reader*? I have often wondered in what guise you would appear or, as it were, what incarnation you would assume."[29]

If not a verbatim, account, it is as parody worthy of another friend of the Sitwells and the Sphinx, Max Beerbohm.

Less gracious than James was another elderly man of letters, George Moore, one of her admirers of many years before. In an appendix to Joseph Hone's *The Life of George Moore,* Moore's cook and housekeeper, Clara Warville, writes of Moore in his last years: "One lady that used to call, her name was Mrs. Ada Leverson, who was very deaf, he gave us orders that when she called again to say that he was out. He had something else to do besides shouting in her ear. What she wanted was an ear trumpet."[30] Mrs. Leverson would probably have been amused both at her old friend's rudeness and at his housekeeper's prose style.

In other brief pictures of the elderly Sphinx like those just given, authors frequently touch on her wit, her gaiety, her unflagging interest in the young. In fact, it is wrong to call her "elderly"; she kept her interest in the young because she was one of them.[31]

Energetic and social as her life was, she still found time to write a few short pieces. There were three stories in the *English Review* between 1919 and 1922, and for T. S. Eliot's *Criterion* in 1926 she wrote some of her memories of Wilde in "The Last First Night," which later constituted part of the introductory essay to *Letters to the Sphinx from Oscar Wilde* in 1930. The *Criterion,* in its alert recognition of new movements in art, philosophy, and so forth, was as significant a periodical to the 1920's and 1930's as the *Yellow Book* had been to the 1890's. It is fitting that her last publication, *Letters to the Sphinx,* concerned her great friend dead so many years. He, if anyone, had begun her career; and with him she ended it.

She was taken ill in Florence in 1933. When she returned to England, pneumonia set in. She rallied enough to move from her hotel to rooms at No. 8, Clarges Street, where her daughter nursed her. She grew worse and died, aged seventy, on August 30, 1933.

## V *Influences and Parallels*

Side by side with the estheticism and decadence of the 1880's and 1890's, wit and comedy flourished. A rococo spirit pervaded everything from house decoration to food to women's clothing; but, at the same time, the era saw the beginning of Max Beerbohm and the heyday of *Punch*. The two tendencies could be combined in the same person: Oscar Wilde, who wrote both *Salomé* and *The Importance of Being Earnest*. There is considerable effeteness in the latter work; but there is no comedy, or none that is intentional, in the former. The excessive modishness of the age, when the chic and the elegant were far more central to the general tenor of the times when they had been in the earlier Victorian period, became an easy target for wit. The fin de siècle overripeness produced its healthy obverse, the chastening astringency of comedy.

Civilized, or overcivilized, London preferred its humor light. Dark comedy had its origins later in World War I. The London of the 1890's responded to the short comic sketch, the caricature, the quip, and the cartoon. We might conclude that wit had not been so highly prized since the Restoration—a period which has other points in common with the end of the nineteenth century. In both periods conversation, especially witty conversation, was an art. The greatest talker of all, as we have noted earlier, was Wilde; and Ada Leverson was known as a wit before she ever wrote a word.

Mrs. Wyndham mentions several musical-hall entertainers and writers, such as Corney Grain, by whose comic style her mother was influenced.[32] Only anecdotes about Corney Grain survive; but the Grossmith brothers, Weedon and George, whom Mrs. Leverson must often have seen on the stage, have left us an example of their comedy in their very popular work *The Diary of a Nobody*,[33] which retains its appeal today. The journal of pompous suburban white-collar worker Charles Pooter, it concerns his small catastrophes and triumphs, his wife Carrie, his friends Gowing and

Cummings, and his reckless son Lupin Pooter. The *Diary* is a technical triumph in its point of view, for behind the self-important but harmless "I" of the narrator, we are privileged to see Mr. Pooter himself. The result is highly ironic. We understand just what he does not understand, laugh at his laughter over his dreadful puns and jokes, see his friends and associates playing pranks on him which he never for a moment takes other than solemnly, and judge how small his great problems and worries actually are.

But we like him. The Grossmiths are closest to Mrs. Leverson in this respect: their satire, like hers, is tolerant. A sly subtlety resides in their presentation of Mr. Pooter, and some philosophy is found in their irony. Mrs. Leverson's ironies are, in her early short pieces, and in the first three of her six novels, usually more immediate than organic, though occasionally some of her characters, in the same way as Pooter, are viewed with consistent irony throughout an entire novel; and these are some of her best characters—Sir James Crofton, M.P., in her first novel, *The Twelfth Hour,* and the magnificient Madame Frabelle in her last, *Love at Second Sight.*

The suburban world of *The Diary of a Nobody* is not one into which the novels of Mrs. Leverson ever venture, but another very popular humorous work of the 1890's is set in her own milieu of upper-class London: *The Dolly Dialogues* of "Anthony Hope" (pseudonym of Sir Anthony Hope Hawkins),[34] best known today as the author of *The Prisoner of Zenda.* His book *The Dolly Dialogues,* however, unlike his romantic *Prisoner of Zenda,* is not in the least dated, and it is easy to share Ada Leverson's liking for this very amusing and very civilized book. Presented principally in the form of dialogue, like her own novels, the novel is composed in short chapters, again like hers, and they have the episodic, quasi-unrelated quality often characteristic of Mrs. Leverson's.

The hero of *The Dolly Dialogues* is Simon Carter, a sophisticated, fortyish bachelor, who is permanently in love with Dolly, Countess of Mickleham, who, though married, remains the effervescent flirt she was as a debutante when Carter had first wooed her. The amount of flirtation and the wit recall Mrs. Leverson's books, but there is sadness in Carter's love for Dolly because it is hopeless, and thus the wit on occasion becomes poignant.

Hope's humor is less robust than Mrs. Leverson's, but he achieves in the entirely likable character of Carter what Mrs. Leverson never quite so succesfully accomplished—a mature, sophisticated, and believably masculine man who is not effete.

Characterization is not Oscar Wilde's strong point, but the facile sketches of people who populate his plays and who speak animatedly, even if they are not alive, are frequently effete. But if Mrs. Leverson's characters sometimes share this trait, it is not here that significant literary parallels between Wilde and the Sphinx are to be discovered. Generally speaking, even if Wilde was the catalyst of his friend's writing career, she is not in any major sense his follower. She may parody him, but, if the distinction can be made, she does not imitate him.

The resemblances between them are numerous, however. Their milieu and their interest in chronicling the fads and foibles of their immediate society are the same. His plays contain witty dialogue, and her witty novels are almost plays. Paradox, epigram, and simple joke or *plaisanterie* abound in both writers, and both are satirists. However, Mrs. Leverson's satire, more human than Wilde's, is governed by a more traditionally humane philosophic outlook. There is not the sting or bite to her wit that there is to his, and her epigrams are more self-amused and indulgent, less bristling and brilliant than his. There is, in fact, little division between Mrs. Leverson herself and the "I" of her novels, as we have observed before—much less than there is between the private and the public Wilde. His pose is highly polished; his persona has a glossy and impermeable finish and, as we also have noted, part of the appeal of Mrs. Leverson's writing lies in its directness and spontaneity.

Comparison with two other important comic writers contemporary with her, the two most widely read today, may also help to isolate her unique qualities: "Saki" (Hector Hugh Munro), who is currently undergoing a revival; and Ronald Firbank, her friend in Florence and London. Exploration of the psychological motifs in Saki is profitable, as critics have recently demonstrated; but our concern is with his comedy. Again, like Anthony Hope and Mrs. Leverson, Saki's stories are dominated by the use of dialogue. His epigrams and paradoxes are endless; for a sample of their flavor, we cite one from "Reginald in Russia": "The Princess always defended a friend's complexion if it was really bad. With her, as with a great many of her sex, charity began at homeliness and did not generally progress much farther."[35] The preciosity of the 1890's survives in Saki's stories, but his first full-length comic work was not published until after the turn of the twentieth century.

Contrasts, however, are more obvious than comparisons. Funny though Saki's stories often are, the tone, in contrast to Mrs. Leverson's, can be flippant, disagreeable, hard, grim, and cynical. While her ridicule is always amiable, his can border on contempt and even cruelty. In matters of form, his surprise endings nowadays seem dated; the events of his stories tend to fall into place at the end with a thud; in fact, his touch is altogether heavier than hers. In his novel *The Unbearable Bassington*, Saki once refers to the Edwardian scene as "an animal world, and a fiercely competitive animal world at that,"[36] and here he means "animal" in the sense of "debased human," for elsewhere in his stories animals are tutelar deities and the bearers or symbols of the mystery and strangeness of life. Mrs. Leverson may once or twice have considered the bestiality of man and the world, but we would guess from her novels that she quickly dismissed the thought. Still another contrast, a not-unrelated one, is that Saki often uses a rural setting and is, at his best, a superb nature writer; but Mrs. Leverson's flowers are usually wired orchids, and her animals are pets.

She is like Ronald Firbank in this respect. If high society is not what Firbank makes it, we could wish it were; because only he can make poetry out of its pomp, exquisiteness, and obscenity. High priest of the rococo absurd, his wit kept him from writing a *Salomé*. Mrs. Leverson's novels are far more conventional than Firbank's, and her sense of the absurd operates on recognizable data. Firbank's is employed at a much greater distance; he went further than almost all other literary artists of his time in arranging the world into art: he completely reshaped it so that his novels surmount the real and become preposterous. Mrs. Leverson still conceives of conduct in an inherited moral framework; but Firbank is essentially modern in that to him the morality of conduct is, as in Joyce or Beckett, a negligible concern. Firbank did not consciously arrive at this position or at any other; he simply followed his tastes where they led him, and they led him a long way from Ada Leverson's world—although it is obvious that he started there—into regions of the perverse, the bizarre, and the supraelegant. Nonetheless, there remains a strong likeness between Firbank and Leverson in their delight in absurdity and in their serene acceptances.

## CHAPTER 2

# *Ada Leverson's London*

### I *Setting and the Novel*

OF the three traditional elements of fiction—plot, character, and setting[1]—the one we talk least about is setting. Plot engages our most primitive interest as readers; a child listening to a fairy story wants to know, "What happens next?" In fairy stories, in epics, and in medieval romances, character is subordinate to plot. For example, the character of Ulysses is an embodiment of certain primary traits, of cunning, bravery, and endurance; but, once our interest is engaged by the grand abstraction of heroism he represents, our concern is with his adventures.

In later forms of fiction, such as the novel, our interest gradually shifted from plot to character; and we tend to judge a nineteenth-century novelist's ability in terms of the "aliveness" of his characters and the validity of the psychologically complex behavior patterns he creates. We remember George Eliot's Maggie Tulliver in *The Mill on the Floss* long after we have forgotten most of the details of her short life, and only as reflections of character are Flaubert's Emma Bovary's deeds recalled. Plot becomes the vehicle to reveal character. The life events of Turgenev's Bazarov in *Fathers and Sons* or of Dostoevsky's Raskolnikov in *Crime and Punishment,* no matter how dramatic, are not so intrinsically interesting as the characters themselves are. With each significant action, willed or unwilled, we turn back to a deeper analysis of the actor himself. Sometimes, perhaps ideally, as Henry James has indicated, out of character stems action; and action in turn shapes character. In this fashion the two are organically fused; and we can say, with the German Romantic philosopher Frederick Novalis, that character *is* destiny.

These comments may not hold in certain striking cases, such as that of Dickens, where character is often flat and plot is incessant. But it is interesting that his *Great Expectations,* the least typical of his major works, is today probably his most discussed novel: the reason may be that, though it has plot enough and to spare, it does not lead us through those bewildering mazes of coincidence which determine the stories of *Bleak House* or *Little Dorrit;* in fact, our attention is focused throughout on character, specifically on the complexly rendered character of Pip. In the case of George Eliot, her novels are sufficiently Victorian to include traditional plot elements like lost documents, misplaced wills, and so forth; but, if she is truly the first modern novelist in English, as she is often said to be, that reputation rests on the authority of her psychology.

In every novel so far referred to, setting is important. What would Dickens be without London, or Turgenev without the Russian countryside? Even in the Brontës, the best examples we can offer of the use of the "pathetic fallacy," scene and person and incident are never so inseparable that our attention can long stray from Lucy Snowe of *Villette* or Heathcliff of *Wuthering Heights* or from the life styles they represent.

In a novel written today—in a "new" novel by Samuel Beckett or Alain Robbe-Grillet, not in the vestigially Victorian books of, say, Angus Wilson—setting seems to remain the hard core of the fictional triad while plot and character have begun to disintegrate. The Malone of Beckett becomes the people in the stories he tells; the outlines of character blur and vanish. There is a basic "I" in Beckett's "novels," but the "I" may be Beckett, it may be one of Beckett's characters, it may be a character that one of Beckett's characters has created, or it may be all three. Malone's stories are neither concluded nor conclusive. The new novel is open-ended, which means that plot trails off, or pauses, or is poised among ambiguities—which may not even be, as they are in Henry James, ambiguities we can accept as final. Even if we are no more "placed" than in a nearly featureless room, or a cabbage field meticulously counted and described, nevertheless, with Beckett, Robbe-Grillet, and new novelists in general, we still are somewhere—the "thereness" is still there; even if our sense of the identity of the narrator is frustrated and what is happening to him is unclear or opaque, he has nearly invariably a locus. Setting survives, therefore, as one familiarity from earlier narrative.

With Ada Leverson, we are light years from Beckett; with her, setting is uniquely recognizable. The means by which it is made recognizable are to be considered, but the point to be made about it here, in connection with those large generalizations which have just been suggested about the role of setting in earlier and later fiction, is that setting is a far more dominant element in her novels than is usual. Novelists always have their geographies, but some may substantiate their settings with as much detail as a cartographer, massively transposing a real world into a fictional world; and we, as readers, become what José Ortega y Gasset called "temporal 'provincials' "[2] of Anthony Trollope's Barsetshire and Thomas Hardy's Wessex and William Faulkner's Yoknapatawpha County. In Ada Leverson's six novels, the locale is London. The rare excursions into the country have a Watteau-like charm, but London is where she is most at home.

Her London is not the big raw city of Henry James's *The Princess Casamassima,* of Joseph Conrad's *The Secret Agent,* of Arnold Bennett's *Riceyman Steps,* or of Muriel Spark's *The Ballad of Peckham Rye;* hers is Edwardian Mayfair—a limitation of scope that provides a rewarding thoroughness of detail. Henry James spoke of the need in a novel for "solidity of specification."[3] The exact notation of street and shop, of the way life is lived at its most quotidian as well as at its climaxes, of the very sight and sound and smell of a place—all these engage our natural curiosity; and all these Ada Leverson, granted always the restrictions of era and milieu, lavishly provides. One can learn more about antebellum life on the Mississippi from Mark Twain's *Huckleberry Finn* than from a score of historical or sociological or economic treatises, and the slightness of Mrs. Leverson's novels is to some extent redeemed by the interest of their setting. Great authorities on almost any subject are interesting.

The relevant esthetic concern is to what degree the details of setting are or are not straight transcriptions of what we call "reality." The Firbank country has undergone a sea change; the locales of Trollope and Hardy and Faulkner, on the other hand, are easily, perhaps meant to be, deciphered: we know that Hardy's Casterbridge is Dorchester, that Trollope's Barchester is both Salisbury and Winchester, and that Faulkner's Jefferson is Oxford, Mississippi. But Ada Leverson in her use of setting is, oddly enough, most like Joyce. The Dublin of *Ulysses* is the Dublin of June 16, 1904. Joyce may have transformed and amalgamated people he knew into characters in his books, but today there are guided tours of what remains, after sixty or seventy years, of Joyce's Dublin, and the plethora of details of the actual Dublin scene is one of the wonders of *Ulysses*. The intrusion of the real world into the world of a novel has been thought by some theorists to be a dangerous invitation to a reader to forget his suspension of disbelief. But, in regard to setting, the reader's imagination is more powerful than such warnings would suggest; in fact, a reader finds it no problem to imagine Joyce's imaginary Leopold Bloom in a real Barney Kiernan's or the imaginary Edith Ottley of Ada Leverson in a real Carlton Hotel.

Mrs. Leverson's London, like Joyce's Dublin, is so solidly and accurately evoked that we, who are not Mayfair Edwardians any more than we are Edwardian Dubliners, have the interest of a certain point in history brought vividly before us through her novels. She herself commented: "One thing remains to be said in favour of accurately realistic novels of the present day. They quickly grow old-fashioned, but if they are well done they remain documents. In about ten years or so—we live quickly nowadays—they become interestingly antique instead of merely antiquated."[4]

## II *The Land of the Little Ottleys*

Ada Leverson's London is the London of those years in which her six novels were published, 1907–16. When she describes the fashions or furniture of an earlier day, such as the 1870's of her girlhood, the 1880's of her early married life, or, especially, the 1890's of her friendship with Wilde, the distinctive features of those periods are never blurred. If an esthetic type of the 1890's, such as Rupert Denison in her *Bird of Paradise*, appears in Edwardian times, the anachronism of such a picture is carefully pointed out (50).[5] Mrs. Leverson had the sense of social change of William M. Thackeray, and she is at least as accurate as he in describing an earlier generation. She lacks, however, his examination into cause, or his melancholy philosophy of history.

One of the peripheral interests of her picture of Edwardian London is to note what has not changed. Society marriages, then as now, often took place at St. George's, Hanover Square (*The Limit*, 180); and, for Roman Catholics, the Brompton Oratory was the most fashionable of churches (*Love at Second Sight*, 231). At the same time that we are struck by how little London has changed in certain respects, the fact that half a century has passed emerges strongly—when we read, for example, that suitable wedding presents were "glass screens painted with storks and water-lilies . . . silver hair-brushes . . . carriage-clocks . . . umbrella-handles and photograph-frames" (*Love's Shadow,* 188–89), or hear Valentia Wyburn, the heroine of *The Limit,* remark, "Love in a cottage is only all right for the weekend when you have a nice house in London as well, and a season ticket or a motor, and electric light and things, and a telephone" (266–67). Telephones were new; cables were called "Marconigrams" (*The Limit,* 183); and, among Mrs. Leverson's characters, the Messenger Boy Service seems to be the type of written communication most often used. A formality of address little known today prevailed: Bertie Wilton, in love with Felicity in *The Twelfth Hour,* still calls her "Lady Chetwode" (223); and the elderly Mrs. Ottley refers to her husband, when talking to her daughter-in-law Edith, as "Mr. Ottley" (*Love's Shadow,* 89). Slang like "You *are* a nut!" (Moona Chivvey in *Bird of Paradise,* 62) sounds dated indeed.

Another instance of that mixture of what has survived and what has not can be found in the references to Edwardian celebrities. A list like the following from *The Twelfth Hour* includes names which are still bright, or half in oblivion, or quite obscure: "Mr. Chamberlain, Beerbohm Tree, Arthur Balfour, Madame Melba, Filsen Young, George Alexander, and Winston Churchill" (90). The American millionaire Van Buren in *The Limit* has, in his "lion hunting," encountered "Bernard Shaw, and Graham White, and Lloyd George, and Thomas Hardy, and Sargent, and Lord Roberts, and Henry James, and even Gabrielle Ray" (118). Everyone today has heard of Duse (*Bird of Paradise,* 259) and Nijinsky (*Tenterhooks,* 45, 55, 64), but few remember very distinctly George Alexander (*The Limit,* 55), Clara Butt (*The Twelfth Hour,* 131), George Grossmith (*Tenterhooks,* 64), or Harry Lauder (*The Limit,* 66).

In *Love at Second Sight,* published in 1916, Charlie Chaplin and Winston Churchill were already among the famous (163). It will be a long time, certainly after Mrs. Leverson's novels have ceased to be read, before such names awaken no echoes; but some of the immediacy of her work has already faded because we lack the degree of conversance earlier readers had. A contemporary reader would have understood at once the reference to Alec, the gauche and appealing girl who is in love with Harry de Freyne in *The Limit*, that she was "named after her distinguished godmother" (59); it is only with an effort that a reader today—at least an American reader—realizes that the allusion is to Princess (later Queen) Alexandra, wife of the monarch that gave his name to the era. On the other hand, there is a certain charm to the dated, especially when what is dated seems part of a more orderly and rational existence than our own. In Mrs. Leverson's novels even references to the forgotten famous are today part of the substantiating believability of her milieu.

Her milieu, as we have suggested, is a limited one; the land of the little Ottleys is confined to Mayfair, that part of London for which the postal district is "W.1" and which is bounded by Oxford Street on the north, Regent Street on the east, Piccadilly on the south, and Park Lane on the west. Among characters for whose houses actual street names in Mayfair are given, there are Chetwode in *The Twelfth Hour*, who lives in Park Street (10); Aunt William, of the same novel, who occupies a "large ugly house in South Audley Street" (40); Bertie Wilton, also in *The Twelfth Hour*, who has a flat in Half Moon Street (262); and Nigel Hillier of *Bird of Paradise*, whose rich wife owns a mansion in Grosvenor Street (63). Others who dwell in or very near Mayfair are Aylmer Ross, hero of *Tenterhooks* and *Love at Second Sight*, who lives at No. 27 Jermyn Street, today a nonexistent address (*Tenterhooks*, 63; *Love at Second Sight*, 264), and the composer in *Love at Second Sight*, Sir Tito Landi, the exact address of whose studio in Mayfair is not given (216).

Knightsbridge, to the southwest of the West End, was also an elegant address. Bertha and Percy Kellynch in *Bird of Paradise* live at No. 100 Sloane Street, now part of the Grosvenor Court Flats, Nos. 97–102 Sloane Street (119). Bruce and Edith Ottley in *Love's Shadow* live in "a very new, very small, very white flat in Knightsbridge—exactly like thousands of other new, small, white flats" (9). By the second novel in which they appear, *Tenterhooks*, the Ottleys' address has been made specific: it is 3 Linden Mansions, Cadogan Square, Knightsbridge (78). They are still in Knightsbridge but are now living on Sloane Street in their third and final appearance in *Love at Second Sight* (14). The most fashionable address in all the novels is perhaps that of the amiable Lady Conroy in *Love at Second Sight*, who lives—as did, at one time, the famous hostess in real life, Lady Cunard—in Carlton House Terrace (246).

One has the impression that regions beyond Mayfair and Knightsbridge were outer darkness. Bloomsbury was perhaps acceptable—the actor Arthur Mervyn in *The Twelfth Hour* lives in "a large, luxuriously furnished flat" in that district (65); but it is to a boardinghouse in Bloomsbury that Anne Yeo, companion to Hyacinth Verney in *Love's Shadow*, banishes herself (222). Kensington, however, comes in for the most adverse commentary as a place of residence. The Aunt William of *The Twelfth Hour* regards the residence of her brother-in-law, Sir James Crofton, in Onslow Square in Kensington as deplorable: "Tell your father I'm sure I shall enjoy his entertainment, though why on *earth* he still lives in Onslow Square, when he ought to be in London, I can't and never shall, understand. However, I believe there's quite a sort of society in Kensington, and no doubt *some* of the right people will be there" (49). If Aunt William will not admit that Kensington is in London, Bruce Ottley in *Love's Shadow* is even more severe. Refusing to drive all the way from his own flat in Knightsbridge to dine with his parents, he protests, "West Kensington. It's off the map. I'm not an explorer—I don't pretend to be" (84).

Hardly any other districts of London than those we have mentioned are referred to. The world of the novels is a few square miles.

### III *The Sinfulness of Sunflowers, and the Folly of Fans*

A Mayfair address does not tell us much about the owner of a house or flat other than that he is fashionable and prosperous, but the interior of a residence, when described, is often used to inform us what its occupant is like as an individual, and thus serves a double purpose. Lord Chetwode in *The Twelfth Hour* has three interests in life: his wife, Felicity; horses; and antiques. He furnishes his house exquisitely with "old French furniture" (10), and the way in which he regards Felicity as simply the finest of his *objets d'art* is shown quite subtly by sentences like "In the bedroom, especially, not a concession was made, not a point stretched. All was purest Louis-Quinze" (10). Chetwode's drawing room would, in some circles, be considered *à la mode* today: "It was a beautiful room with hardly anything in it; a large, high, empty room in pure First Empire style. A small yellow sofa with gilded claws, and narrow bolster cushions, was near the fireplace; a light blue curved settee, with animals' heads, was in the middle of the room. There was a highly polished parquet floor with no carpet, a magnificent chandelier, and the curtains were held up by elaborately carved and gilded cornices with warlike ornament" (203).

A typical drawing room of the period, however, contained "fat cushions, unnecessary draperies, photographs, and vases of flowers" (*The Twelfth Hour,* 203–4). Lady Cannon's "magnificent" drawing room in *Love's Shadow* is typical of the very rich: "It was so high, so enormous, with so much satin on the walls, so many looking-glasses, so much white paint, so many cabinets full of Dresden china . . ." (172). Lady Everard's music room in *Tenterhooks* is as cluttered as the mind of that foolish lady with "quantities of signed photographs in silver frames . . . large waste-paper baskets, lined with blue satin and trimmed with pink rosettes . . . fans which were pockets, stuffed cats which were paperweights, oranges which were pincushions, and other debris from the charitable and social bazaars of which she was a constant patroness" (217). Both untypical and surprising is the drawing room of the odd and avant-garde Miss Belvoir in *Bird of Paradise.* It is "furnished in a Post-Impressionist style, chiefly in red, black, and brown; the colours were all plain—that is to say, there were no designs except on the ceiling, which was cosily covered with large, brilliantly tinted, life-sized parrots" (257).

To return again to Aunt William in *The Twelfth Hour,* the description of her house, one of the fullest in all the novels, is an exact rendering of her amusing conservatism; but the passage also shows the accuracy in period detail that we have earlier credited to Mrs. Leverson:

> If there were a certain charm in the exterior of this old house—solid and aggressively respectable—its interior gave most visitors at first a nervous shock. Aunt William still believed aestheticism to be fashionable, and a fad that should be discouraged. Through every varying whim of the mode she had stuck, with a praiseworthy persistence, to the wax flowers under glass, Indian chessmen, circular tables in the centre of the room, surrounded by large books, and the rep curtains (crimson, with grey borders) of pre-artistic days. Often she held forth to wondering young people, for whom the 1880 fashions were but an

echo of ancient history, on the sad sinfulness of sunflowers and the fearful folly of Japanese fans. Had the poor lady been a decade or two more old-fashioned she would have been considered quaint and up-to-date. (A narrow escape, had she only known it!) (41)

Her niece Felicity also describes the house, with malice and exclamation points: "And you know the house. Wax flowers under glass, rep curtains. And the decorations on the table! A strip of looking-glass, surrounded by smilax! And the dinner! Twelve courses, port and sherry—all the fashions of 1860, or a little later, which is worse. Not mahogany and walnuts. Almonds and raisins!" (159).

Edith Ottley is Mrs. Leverson's favorite heroine. The style of her drawing room, which reflects Edith's "cultured and quiet taste" (*Love at Second Sight*, 44), may be taken as Mrs. Leverson's ideal, since Edith is clearly a projection, fantasy, or wish fulfillment of Ada. In *Love's Shadow* (1908), we read of "the neat white room with its miniature overmantel, pink walls, and brass fire-irons like toys . . . frail white chairs . . . diminutive white writing-desk . . . the ceiling . . . painted in imitation of a blue sky . . . " (202). By the time of *Tenterhooks* (1912), Edith seems to enjoy monochromatic effects: "almost everything in the room . . . was green, except the small white enamelled piano" (103). In the last novel, *Love at Second Sight* (1916), in which Edith has attained the status of pure paragon, her house contains "dull greys and blues, and surfaces without design" (44); her drawing room is "soft and subdued in colour"; it has "shaded lights" (47–48). Her great friend, the composer Sir Tito Landi, also has a "*laqué* white" piano, and the furniture of his studio, "extremely luxurious and comfortable, was in colour a pale and yet dull pink" (216). From Lord Chetwode's drawing room in *The Twelfth Hour* to Edith's in *Love at Second Sight*, we can see what standards of cultured and quiet taste Mrs. Leverson upheld; and we may also note that these standards, where they still exist, have not much changed today.

## IV *The Elegant Quotidian*

The inhabitants of Mrs. Leverson's Mayfair visit one another and make their rounds of business and pleasure in a variety of means of transportation. Photographs of London Bridge in the early years of the present century show an astonishing range of conveyance, from small horse-drawn carriage to huge horse-drawn two-decker omnibus, from bicycle to stately Humber limousine. Automobiles—usually called "motors"—were both gas and electric propelled, and they came in many shapes and sizes. Rich amateurs even designed their own, as Bertie Wilton in *The Twelfth Hour* tells us: "Broughton . . . has actually invented a car of his own . . . but it seems to me that it isn't an ideally convenient arrangement (particularly for ladies) to have to climb into a motor, by means of a ladder, over the back! I understood that though Broughton's design had all sorts of capital new arrangements with regard to cushions and clocks and looking-glasses, and mudguards, he had, *most* unfortunately, quite forgotten the door" (73).

Lord Chetwode says of Bertie that he is "a boy who rattles about in a staring red motor-car. How any one on earth can stand those things when they can have horses———" (168). Chetwode would undoubtedly approve of his wife's Aunt William, who can still be seen on Bond Street "in her old-fashioned barouche with grey horses" (79). From comments here and there in the novels, it is clear that the triumph of the automobile was already assured (see, for example, *Tenterhooks,* 214); taxis and hansoms were both current, but hansoms were on their way out, and soon enough the only horses to be seen in London were those of mounted policemen or those ridden by the rich on the bridlepaths of Hyde Park.

It is surprising how many of the shops and other places of business of Ada Leverson's London survive today. Aunt William in her barouche may have been on her way to the famous firm of Charbonnel and Walker at No. 31 Old Bond Street to buy chocolates for her beloved nephew Savile (see also *Bird of Paradise,* 127). It was Christie's for auctions (*The Twelfth Hour,* 158), Chappell's at No. 50 New Bond Street for sheet music (*The Twelfth Hour,* 80), Hatchards of Piccadilly for books (*The Twelfth Hour,* 282), Liberty's for the finest fabrics (*Love's Shadow,* 21), Cook's for travel arrangements (*Love's Shadow,* 300), and Boots' for almost anything (*Tenterhooks,* 235). Waring's is mentioned half a dozen times as famous for furniture, but the two leading department stores were already Harrod's, in Knightsbridge, and Selfridge's, that huge Oxford Street monument to Edwardian prosperity. The elder Mrs. Ottley in *Love's Shadow* says what many a matron today might say: "I'm going to Harrod's, of course. I'm always going to Harrod's; it's the only place I ever do go" (185). When Rupert Denison in *Bird of Paradise* learns that Madeline Irwin sometimes buys her hats at Selfridge's, he jokes, "Oh, I didn't know you were a Selfridgette!" (53). Aylmer Ross in *Tenterhooks* suggests "a great cricket match when the shopping season's over between the Old Selfridgians, and the Old Harrodians . . ." (236). Mrs. Leverson almost always employs the names of actual establishments for her characters to shop in, and they seem to be much busier shopping than are characters in other novels. Women, of course, spend more time than men in shopping, and Ada Leverson's matrons, like Virginia Woolf's, are busy buying this or that.

Another detail which gives the novels their accent of a kind of daily veracity is the frequent reference to restaurants. Naturally, Willis's in King Street—Ada Leverson's and Oscar Wilde's own favorite—is mentioned most frequently; indeed, the title of Chapter IX of *The Twelfth Hour* is called "A Dinner at Willis's." The other two most popular dining establishments, mentioned over and over, are the Carlton and the Savoy. For example, in *Bird of Paradise,* the party of Bertha Kellynch, Nigel Hillier, Madeline Irwin, and Rupert Denison meet in the Palm Court of the Carlton, dine at the Carlton, attend the Russian Ballet, and then go to the Savoy for supper (93). The Carlton, near Trafalgar Square, has now disappeared; but the Savoy still reigns in the Strand. Rumpelmeyer's has also disappeared from London (though not from Paris); Chapter IV of *Bird of Paradise,* "Rupert at Rumpelmeyer's," shows the popularity of that establishment for tea among West End people of fashion.

If women have their shopping, men have their clubs and other means of entertainment. Lord Chetwode, in *The Twelfth Hour,* is a member of White's (170); and Woodville, in the same novel, dines at another club, unspecified (185). In *Bird of Paradise,* Percy Kellynch has two "mild hobbies"—one is "squash rackets at the Bath Club" and the other "took the form of Tschaikovsky at the Queen's Hall" (14). Gentlemen went to Lord's for cricket (*Bird of Paradise,* 28) and attended race meetings like Kempton, Doncaster, and the Cambridgeshire (*Love at Second Sight,* 186; and elsewhere).

Other amusements of a noncultural type—the pleasures of culture are discussed in a later section of the present chapter—

are parties, games, and expeditions to Madame Tussaud's. Aunt William in *The Twelfth Hour* is once again our authority on what was or was not *au courant:* "Aunt William resented automobiles as much as she disliked picture postcards, week-ends, musical comedies, and bridge" (43). The slang term for a party was a "beano"; and someone who spoiled a party was a "beano-blighter" (*The Limit*, 237). Fancy-dress balls were frequent: Chapter VIII, "In Fancy Dress," of *The Limit* concerns one; and Bertie Wilton mentions one in *The Twelfth Hour*, adding, "I went as Louis the Nineteenth" (74). In the same novel, Chapter XV is called "Madame Tussaud's," and Mrs. Leverson's description of that museum is one of her liveliest: "The party met fairly punctually in the hideous hall, furnished with draughts and red velvet. The gloom was intensified by the sound of an emaciated orchestra playing 'She was a Miller's Daughter,' with a thin reckless airiness that was almost ghostly" (p. 178).

By far the most popular game is a word game called "Dumb Crambo." Another was "Diabolo." Others include charades, tableaux vivants, and "Consequences." Fads included palmistry (see especially Chapter XX of *The Twelfth Hour*, "Zero, the Soothsayer") and Sandow's exercises, which both Bruce Ottley *(Tenterhook*, 13) and Leopold Bloom in *Ulysses* have attempted.

An accurate if brief history of the dance in these years can be traced in the novels. Old-fashioned Lady Kellynch, in *Bird of Paradise*, does not take lessons in the tango, or learn skiing, or roller-skating (210). But everyone young did the tango. In fact, when Madeline Irwin in *Bird of Paradise* is proposed to by Charlie Hillier, her main reason for accepting him is: that " 'He dances the tango so beautifully; I think it all came through that. We got on so splendidly at tango teas . . . .' 'It's a tango marriage,' said Bertha" (158). Other dances mentioned in *Bird of Paradise*, which was published in 1914, are the two-step, one-step, and the "double-Boston" (16). At the time of *Tenterhooks*, published in 1912, the American two-step and the Turkey Trot were the rage (155), and in *Love at Second Sight*, published in 1916, the popular step is the fox-trot (178).

## V *Clothes*

Violet Wyndham tells us that one of her mother's dresses was "a white chiffon tea gown edged with sable, costing forty guineas;

a prodigious sum then . . . ."[6] The portraits of Mrs. Leverson show her in exquisite dresses, and the column she wrote for the *Referee* from 1903 to 1905 is full of references to the latest French, English, and American modes. This interest in style is carried over almost excessively into the novels; at its most interesting, just as in the case of interior decoration, the costume reflects the wearer. For an example, we have Lady Cannon of *Love's Shadow*, most dreadful of dowagers in 1908 but a former belle of the 1880's; like other matrons in the novels, she wears a "royal fringe" —inspired by Princess Alexandra. It is one of Mrs. Leverson's most brilliant descriptions:

> Lady Cannon had never been seen after half-past seven except in evening dress, generally a velvet dress of some dark crimson or bottle-green, so tightly-fitting as to give her an appearance of being rather upholstered than clothed. Her cloaks were always like well-hung curtains, her trains like heavy carpets; one might fancy that she got her gowns from Gillows [a furnisher's]. Her pearl dog-collar, her diamond ear-rings, her dark red fringe and the other details of her toilette were put on with the same precision when she dined alone with Sir Charles as if she were going to a ceremonious reception. She was a very tall, fine-looking woman. In Paris, where she sometimes went to see Ella [her daughter] at school, she attracted much public attention as *une femme superbe*. Frenchmen were heard to remark to one another that her husband *ne devrait pas s'embêter* (which, as a matter of fact, was precisely what he did—to extinction); and even in the streets when she walked out the gamins used to exclaim, "*Voilà l'Arc de Triomphe qui se promène!*"—to her intense fury and gratification. (34–35)

Lady Cannon, when especially out of temper, wears a good deal of shiny jet (286). At Hyacinth Verney's wedding, she wears a mauve toque and an embroidered velvet gown; and she is so tightly corseted that her daughter Ella exclaims admiringly, "You look lovely, Mamma—as though you couldn't breathe!" (188). Another belle of the 1880's is Lady Kellynch in *Bird of Paradise*: "Lady Kellynch had had a success in 1887; she cherished tenderly a photograph of herself in an enormous bustle, with an impossibly small waist, a thick high fringe over her eyes, and a tight dog-collar. The bald bare look about the ears, and the extraordinary figure resembling a switchback made her look very much older then than she did now" (211).

We know from Mrs. Wyndham that her mother patronized the establishment of Paquin on Dover Street;[7] he is mentioned, always as the epitome of *haute couture,* a dozen times in the novels, and is lavishly patronized by rich women younger than the ladies Cannon and Kellynch. Felicity Chetwode's instructions to her maid in *The Twelfth Hour* may be taken as typical, in a general way, of what an elegant young matron would wear: "Everett, I'll wear my tailor-made dress this morning and for lunch. The mauve tea-gown at four. I'm only going to the theatre to-night. Let me see, what is it? Oh! the St. James's. The white *crêpe de chine*" (102–3).

If such passages sound a little too like a lady's journal, Mrs. Leverson is in better form when she is describing lapses in taste. For example, we have the description of Lady Virginia's disastrous attire in *The Twelfth Hour:* "a limp crêpe de chine Empire Gown of an undecided mauve, with a waist under the arms and puffed sleeves. On her head was a very smart bright blue flower toque, put on entirely wrong, with a loose blue veil hanging at the back. Had anything been required to decide the question of her looking grotesque, I should mention that she wore long mauve *suède* gloves. That settled it. A gold bag dangled from her left wrist, and she carried a little fan of carved ivory. She looked, naturally,—or unnaturally—slightly absurd . . ." (294). Even more adversely critical is the description of "artistic" Moona Chivvey's garb in *Bird of Paradise:*

> When I say that she had handsome regular aquiline features, two thick curtains of black hair drawn over her ears, from which depended long ear-rings of imitation coral, it seems almost unnecessary to add (for this type of girl always dresses in the same way), that she wore a flat violet felt hat, the back of which touched her shoulders, a particularly tight dark blue serge coat and skirt, a very low collar, and lisle thread stockings which showed above low shiny shoes with white spats. In her hands she held a pair of new white gloves, unworn. (58–59)

Bertha Kellynch says of poor vulgar Miss Chivvey:

> "I don't think Miss Chivvey's dangerous, seriously. She uses cheap scent."
>
> "Oh!" cried Madeline, delighted. "There's nothing so awful as cheap scent."
>
> "Except expensive scent, because it's stronger," said Bertha. (98)

For a final example of stylistic abominations, Mrs. Leverson presents Mrs. Pickering in *Bird of Paradise,* now a millionaire *arriviste,* formerly a soubrette. Young Clifford Kellynch, who adores Mrs. Pickering, describes her, to his mother's horror, in "an awful ripping violet sort of dress, and violet satin boots with fur round the edge . . ." (217). When she arrives at Lady Kellynch's for tea, Mrs. Pickering "spoke with a very slight Cockney accent . . . [she] bristled with aigrettes and sparkled with jewels. Her bodice was cut very low, her sleeves very short, and her white gloves came over the braceleted elbows. She wore a very high, narrow turban, green satin shoes and stockings, and altogether was dressed rather excessively; she looked like one of Louis Bauer's drawings in *Punch*" (219).

Styles changed, and do change, so rapidly, that no ideal composite of the well-dressed young woman can be derived from the novels, even though they were written within a space of nine or ten years. Empire dresses seem to have been the rage in 1907 and 1908 (*The Twelfth Hour,* 294; *Love's Shadow,* 89); and for that same period Bertie Wilton in *The Twelfth Hour* tells us what hats were like. There were two extremes: one, "the most enormous hat, eccentric beyond the dreams of the Rue de la Paix, all feathers"; and the other, "those absurd, tiny, high, little things that require at least twenty-five imitation curls to keep them up . . ." (78). But we must once again turn to the model woman, Edith Ottley, for hints of what Mrs. Leverson considered the highest style. For a first night, Edith is going to have a dress of Liberty satin—it "wears better than Nattier's' "—in " 'that new shade of blue' " (*Love's Shadow,* 141). Insisting on simplicity in her clothes, she instructs her faithful friend, Miss Bennett, who shops for her, to find some "perfectly simple" teagowns made "rather like evening cloaks"; to wear with them, she wants "just one very large black velvet orchid" (*Tenterhooks,* 100, 101). Edith is not perfectly conventional; for instance, as her lover Aylmer Ross remarks, she wears gray gloves, not white ones; she explains, "I prefer white ones, but they won't stay white two minutes" (*Love at Second Sight,* 236).

Of men's clothes, we learn little; but there was little to learn. The major change in men's clothing during the Edwardian era, someone has said, was that white evening waistcoats changed from being rounded at the waist to pointed. The 1890's had been a period of some little experimentation and fancifulness in men's clothes, and Rupert Denison in *Bird of Paradise,* an example of "the rather old-world dandyism of a past generation," wears a buttonhole of violets to match his violet socks, and "invariably carried a black ebony stick, with an ivory handle" (50); but he does not seem very daring. Boutonnieres were generally worn, and the eccentric Raggett, Bruce Ottley's friend in *Love's Shadow,* even wears one of orchids (75). Matthew Van Buren, the rich young American in *The Limit,* wears Parma violets but denies that he is "a Gibson man" (33). At Lord Selsey's musical afternoon in *Love's Shadow,* "smooth-haired young men in coats that went in at the waist . . ." were present (77). Mrs. Leverson, despite her keen observation of fashion, says so little of men's clothing—except for their boutonnieres—that she may well have believed what many an Englishman still believes: the best-dressed man is the one dressed with perfect unobtrusiveness.

## VI *Culture*

Edith Ottley, as omnivorous a reader as she is remarkable in other respects, tells her lover Aylmer Ross in *Tenterhooks* that she reads "Four morning papers—never mind their names—four evening papers; five Sunday papers: the *Academy,* the *Saturday Review,* the *Bookman,* the *World,* the *English Review.*" When Aylmer asks her if she reads the *Queen, Home Notes,* or the *Tatler*—magazines devoted to the "blue blood" and its rituals—Edith replies, with some malice, that she does indeed buy them but for Bruce, her husband. For Archie, her son, she buys *Chums* and *Little Folks.* And with characteristically conventional unconventionality, Edith also reads *Rhythm,* the little magazine for new poetry, edited by Katherine Mansfield and J. Middleton Murry in 1911–12 (106–7).

Edith must have read newspapers and magazines for several hours a day, and Mrs. Leverson, with her own background as a journalist, emphasizes this aspect of Edwardian culture. Her characters never stop reading, whether it is the precocious young schoolboy Clifford Kellynch in *Bird of Paradise,* whose mother thinks works like Rudyard Kipling's *The Jungle Book* suitable for him but who himself prefers the *English Review* (122), or Madame Frabelle in *Love at Second Sight,* for whom Bruce Ottley buys, to be read on a brief train journey, the *Gentlewoman,* the *World*, the *Field, Punch,* and the *London Mail* (409). Miss Winter, "a young girl with red hair and eager eye-glasses" in *The Twelfth Hour*, says, "I'm interested in things . . . I read all the serious magazines and things, the *Bookman* and the *Saturday Review* and the *Sketch;* and so on" (89). Among newspapers, the *Morning Post*, where engagements were announced, and the *Daily Mail* are mentioned several times (*The Twelfth Hour*, 260; *Love at Second Sight*, 202); and among magazines, *Punch* and the *English Review* would seem to be the most frequently cited (*Love at Second Sight*, 130, 146).

A common feature of daily journals, which has today almost disappeared, is what Mrs. Leverson always calls "feuilletons": sentimental or romantic stories in installments that creep along like a soap opera from day to day. They are the kind of reading that Gerty MacDowell, heroine of the Nausicaa episode in Joyce's *Ulysses*, feeds her passions on; they are also the favorite reading of Dulcie Clay, the devoted young nurse of Aylmer Ross in *Love at Second Sight* (182); and Aylmer himself is once described as "a man of sense, and not an impossible hero in a feuilleton" *(Tenterhooks*, 175). Perhaps the most interesting aspect of these serial tales, which are often mentioned by Mrs. Leverson, is the contrast their garrulous sentimentality supplies to the tougher Romanticism of Mrs. Leverson's own love stories. Part of the popularity of her novels can perhaps be explained by the fact that they were *not* feuilletons, though in certain aspects they are, as we shall see, akin to them. What her novels have that the feuilletons have not is wit and depth; and what they have, that she is entirely devoid of, is melodrama.

Despite all this ephemeral reading, Mrs. Leverson's characters still manage to find a little time for books; and, as in the case of periodicals, the books they read indicate the taste of the times. Famous names float through the pages: G. B. Shaw and J. M. Barrie (*Love's Shadow*, 138), or G. K. Chesterton (*Love at Second Sight*, 247), or Thomas Hardy (*The Limit*, 15), or Maurice Maeterlinck (*The Twelfth Hour*, 27). Edith Ottley, in what is perhaps her only lapse from taste, wishes to give her newborn daughter a name out of Maeterlinck—"Ygraine, or Ysolyn—something like that" (*Tenterhooks*, 10). Usually the references to contemporary writers are satiric; for example, Valentia Wyburn, the heroine of *The Limit*, is going to "read a lot of serious books" during a stay in the country: "H. G. Wells, and Hichens, and Aristotle . . ." (119). Mrs. Foster, mother of Daphne de Freyne's Guardsman lover Cyril in *The Limit,* was once herself a poet; and her slim volume—*Fireflies of Fancy*—was written "very much under the influence of the Passionate School—Swinburne, Rossetti, Ella Wheeler Wilcox, and so on . . ." (52). Mrs. Leverson admired the novels of Henry James,[8] and in *The Twelfth Hour* a curious writer named "Henry Arthur James" is mentioned, apparently a compound of Henry James and Arthur Wing Pinero: "He writes all those books that no one can understand—and those clever plays, you know, that every one goes to see" (88). The most interesting literary reference in the novels is to Wilde. There is only one, and it is found, perhaps significantly, in the last of the novels, *Love at Second Sight,* published in 1916. When Aylmer Ross is comparing the esthetes of the World War I period to those of the 1890's, someone says, "The modern poseurs aren't as good as the old ones. Odle is not so clever as Beardsley. . . ." Aylmer answers, "Of course not. Beardsley had the gift of line—though he didn't always know where to draw it—but his illustrations to Wilde's work were unsuitable, because Beardsley wanted everything down in black and white, and Wilde wanted everything in purple and gold. But both had their restraints, and their pose was reserve, not flamboyance" (115–16). A close friend of Mrs. Leverson's in later life, Reginald Turner, is the author of a novel called *Count Florio and Phillis K.,* which is referred to in passing in *The Limit* (263). As in this instance, the references to other novelists usually have a personal bias or attitude involved.

Far more important than books as a cultural pursuit of Mrs. Leverson's character was the theater. Mrs. Leverson's characters, as some of the quotations from her novels have already shown, are indefatigable theatergoers, whether to a first night at the St. James's Theatre or to a new revue—such as the (imaginary) *You Shut Up* and the one mentioned by Nigel Hillier: "Why not go to the new Revue—'*That will be Fourpence*'—where they have the two young Simultaneous Dancers, the Misses Zanie and Lunie LeFace—one, I fancy, is more simultaneous than the other, I forget which . . ." (*Bird of Paradise,* 26, 35). The St. James's is the most popular "legitimate" theater for Mrs. Leverson's characters, but they also attend the Haymarket, His Majesty's, and the Society Theatres (*Love's Shadow,* 138; *Tenterhooks,* 111). The

Pavilion was already popular for lighter theater and vaudeville (*Bird of Paradise*, 304), as was the Empire where Aylmer Ross's son Teddy, home on leave from the front, relaxes (*Love at Second Sight*, 233); and most famous of all is the Gaiety (*The Twelfth Hour*, 129, 161), which is known to readers of the immortal Daisy Ashford as the "Gaierty." The first two of these three still exist.

It was the age of the great actor-managers and producers, such as Charles Hawtrey, Mrs. Leverson's favorite; George Alexander, at the St. James's; and Mrs. Leverson's special friend, the half-brother of Max—Beerbohm Tree (*Love's Shadow*, 138, 194). Celebrated actresses and entertainers mentioned are Zena Dare (*The Twelfth Hour*, 51) and Cissie Loftus and Julia Neilson (*The Limit*, 57). Bertha Kellynch in *Bird of Paradise* has an interesting reaction to the Russian Ballet, as popular in the Edwardian era as today: "One wants to see it, one is interested, from curiosity, and then, afterwards, there's a sort of Dead Sea-fruitish, sour-grapes, autumn-leaves, sort of feeling! It's too remote from real life and yet it hasn't an uplifting effect. At any rate it always depresses me" (108). Bertha's second sentence, when considered closely, is wonderfully ambiguous, both in its implied esthetics and in the comment quite unconsciously made about Edwardian proprieties and Edwardian "real life."

Of all the seven arts, music in the liveliest in Mrs. Leverson's novels. Current fads in music, vagaries of taste, and the ups and downs of the musical marketplace are given with great alertness and humor, from *The Twelfth Hour* of 1907, where the sixteen-year-old Savile has a noble passion for Adelina Patti—who would have been sixty-four at the time (19: "Oh, the way she sings 'Comin through the Rye!' She's simply—well, ripping's the only word!") to *Love at Second Sight* of 1916, where we meet the "pale, good-looking, too well-dressed, disquieting" young Guy (sometimes called Arthur) Coniston, who "was rather useful in society, being musical and very polite." Coniston, one of the most Firbankian of Mrs. Leverson's people, recalls for example Winsome Brookes in Firbank's *Vainglory*: "Being so young, so pale, and so contemporary, one expected him [Guy Coniston] to sing thin, elusive music by Debussy, Fauré, or Ravel. He seemed never to have heard of these composers, but sang instead threatening songs, such as 'I'll sing thee Songs of Araby!' or defiant, teetotal melodies, like 'Drink to Me only with thine Eyes!' " (50).

Two similar young men are encountered at Lord Selsey's musical afternoon in *Love's Shadow:* "The two young geniuses, George Ranger and Nevil Butt, had just given their rather electrifying performance, one playing the compositions of the other, and then both singing Fauré together, and a small band of Green Bulgarians were now playing strenuously a symphony of Richard Strauss . . ." (77). Absurd as this performance of Strauss might be, the scatterbrained Lady Virginia in *The Twelfth Hour* describes an equally preposterous rendition of a Strauss song by a new singer named Delestin: "Certainly a very enervating song, I must own that—he simply fainted at the piano, and had to be taken away" (295).

Another music-loving enthusiastic lady is Lady Everard in *Tenterhooks:*

> She stopped and held up her small beaded fan, "what's that the band's playing? I know it so well; everyone knows it; it's either *Pagliacci* or *Bohème,* or *some*thing. No, isn't it really? What is it? All the old Italian operas are coming in again, by the way, you know, my dear . . . *Rigoletto, Lucia, Traviata*—the *bel canto*—that sort of thing; there's nothing like it for showing off the voice. Wagner's practically gone out (at least what *I* call out), and I always said Debussy wouldn't last." (129)

Inaccurate in these comments as in everything, Lady Everard's remarks about Wagner and Debussy are contradicted by other references to their popularity. And she herself has forgotten that earlier she had described one of her "Musical Evenings" with "We have all the stars in the season at times—dear Melba and Caruso—and darling Bemberg and dear Debussy! Oh! don't laugh at my enthusiasm, my dear . . ." (89). Even the traditonal anti-Wagnerian makes his appearance in the novels when Lord Chetwode in *The Twelfth Hour* asks his wife Felicity, "Aren't we going to the opera, or something?," and she replies:

> "Is it great agony for you to sit out Wagner?" She showed real sympathy. "It's Tannhäuser, you know."
>
> "Can't say I'm keen about it," he answered, in a depressed voice. (170)

Puccini's popularity was constant throughout the period; and, in addition to Lady Everard's mention of *La Bohème,* we also have a reference to *Madame Butterfly* (*The Twelfth Hour* 94). These mentions assume added interest because of the composer's romantic attachment to Mrs. Leverson's sister, the beautiful Sybil Seligman.[9]

The final art much discussed in the novels is painting. Colin MacInnes, in his introduction to *The Little Ottleys*,[10] admires Mrs. Leverson's talent for being well ahead of the times in her appreciation of the new art movements which the beginning of the twentieth century saw. However, Mrs. Leverson's opinions, though they always show her intelligence and perceptiveness and inquisitiveness, are noncommittal at some times, at others satiric, and occasionally quite negative. For example, her hero Aylmer Ross in *Love at Second Sight* dismisses the large and important movement of Futurism rather smugly (115); earlier, in *Bird of Paradise*, the author caricatures the movement in the foolish person of an Italian Futurist (who at least has a funny name: Semolini): "It is ze entire liberation from the laws of logical perspective that makes movement—the Orphic cubism—if you will allow me to say so!" (86). Aylmer seems to prefer Post-Impressionism, though once again his comments are to an extent dismissive; much more directly, Miss Westbury, a character in *The Limit*, describes to her friend Mrs. Wyburn her reactions when she attended a Post-Impressionist show at the Grafton:

> ". . . A daub and a splash—no real trouble taken—and then you're expected to rave about it. There's one man—some one wants me to buy a picture of his—he paints all his pictures in tiny squares of different colours; when you're close you can't see anything, but it seems that if you walk five feet away it forms into a kind of pattern. It seems it's the tessellated school, and they tell me that in a few years nothing else will count. And what I thought was a mountain in a mist turns out to be 'A Nun with cows grazing.' Silly nonsense I call it!"
>
> "Was the nun grazing, or the cows?" asked Mrs. Wyburn. (90)

Even though Miss Westbury's comments are intended to be comedy rather than criticism, we sense a certain skepticism in Mrs. Leverson herself.

How alert she was to the avant-garde is once again shown in her description of the esthetic Vincy's rooms in *Tenterhooks:* they were "covered with pictures by Futurists and Cubists, wild studies by wild men from Tahiti and a curious collection of savage ornaments and weapons" (92). Generally speaking, and judging from the tone of what evidence there is in the novels, we could assume that the painters Mrs. Leverson preferred were of the last or the last-but-one generation. James Abbott McNeill Whistler and John Singer Sargent are mentioned several times, and admiringly; for example, the heroine of *The Twelfth Hour,* Felicity Chetwode, resembles a pastel, and has "the vagueness, remoteness, and delicacy of a Whistler . . ." (195). The work of the Pre-Raphaelites was still highly regarded; Valentia Wyburn, heroine of *The Limit,* is "the type loved by Rossetti and Burne-Jones" (21) and is compared to the latter painter's "Love Among the Roses" (34).

Mrs. Leverson's characters visit art galleries and exhibitions as assiduously as they attend concerts and the theater. They go to the London Group and the New English (*Love at Second Sight,* 228), the Goupil (*Bird of Paradise,* 228), the Grosvenor in Bond Street (*Bird of Paradise,* 135), and the Carfax in Ryder Street, which had been founded by Mrs. Leverson's close friend Robert Ross (*Love's Shadow,* 251). Mrs. Leverson's gives a fine, sharp description of an exhibition at the Carfax of caricatures by another of her friends, Max Beerbohm: "People's spirits were naturally raised at the sight of the cruel distortions, ridiculous situations, and fantastic misrepresentations of their friends and acquaintances on the walls" (*Love's Shadow,* 251–52). A visit to the Royal Academy by Edith Ottley, Miss Bennett, and Aylmer Ross in *Tenterhooks* quickly produces "Academy headache" as a result of the "acres of oil paintings and dozens of portraits of Chief Justices" (236).

Our long account of the daily activities of Mrs. Leverson's people suggests certain considerations. If some of their pursuits seem, on examination, shallow, we must ask if our own are any better; for elegance is not the most harmful of life styles. Their attraction to culture is individual and real; its vigor is not, finally, vitiated by mere fashion, though fashion enters ubiquitously into their enthusiasms. We note the absence of the moral earnestness with which the earnest Victorians had regarded culture, and conclude that culture for Mrs. Leverson's Edwardians was simply, and rather beautifully, pleasure. Today the picture of her worldlings has taken on a patina; we could not be like them if we would.

Certainly an authentic note is struck when Mrs. Leverson tells us what her people did, what they wore, where they lived, and where they shopped and dined. Her plots sometimes halt, or are forgotten, for a tableaulike effect of a musical afternoon at Lord Selsey's or a dinner party at the Mitchells'. Once again, the shrewdness of her social observation is one of her primary appeals. And the delight with which she made and recorded her observations is contagious; it effects our easy entrance into her London.

## CHAPTER 3

# *Minor Works, 1892–1897*

"WHY don't you collect your wonderful, witty, delightful sketches—so slight, so suggestive, so full of 'esprit' and intellectual sympathy?"[1] Oscar Wilde wrote to Mrs. Leverson as early as 1893. Not only were her sketches never collected, by Mrs. Leverson or anyone else, but also they have never been comprehensively listed, described, and commented upon critically. As later chapters indicate, her six novels and their reissues received wide critical attention; however, since the purpose of this and the following chapter is to attempt, for the first time, as inclusive a survey as possible of everything beside the novels that she wrote, it will be necessary to quote from these minor works at what might otherwise be considered unjustifiable length.

Mrs. Wyndham, in contrast to Wilde's opinion, has said of her mother's weekly articles in the *Referee,* discussed in the following chapter, that they are "of no literary value."[2] Mrs. Wyndham's comment might also be applied to some of the earlier sketches, parodies, and stories. Indeed much of Mrs. Leverson's work before she published her first novel in 1907 is difficult to categorize as journalism or as journalism merging into literature; and it is equally difficult to determine if it is of such literary value that it deserves being collected, as Wilde suggested.

In any case the short pieces, whatever their merit in themselves, have the same interest that has been assigned the novels in the preceding chapter: in them, Ada Leverson's London comes to life just as topically and immediately as it does in the novels. An incisive and energetic social commentator, she shows in her very first published work the born skill of the anatomist. Another interest of her minor pieces is the light they cast on the novels. Like most writers, she repeated herself; she was not one to drop a successful *mot.* What amused her once was likely to amuse her again, so that we find jokes, phrases, situations, and even characters making a return engagement in the novels after a trial run in *Black and White* or *Punch.*

Although the present survey of the minor works is, as has already been stated, intended to be "comprehensive," it is comprehensive only in the sense that it includes everything I could locate.[3] Wilde's letter itself, quoted at the beginning of this chapter, suggests that there were already enough sketches to be collected, but I know of only two or three—in *Black and White* and *Punch*—as early as Wilde's letter, 1893; therefore, we cannot even guess about how much may have been lost. Contributions to periodicals like *Punch* were unsigned, and patient paging through the periodicals of the 1890's like *St. Stephen's Review*—Mrs. Wyndham says that "Meeting Wilde had been an event which restored Ada's good spirits and inspired her to write several stories for *Black and White* and *St. Stephen's Review*"[4]—usually yields nothing certain. How many bright little squibs, tossed off by Mrs. Leverson in a moment and published by *Punch* for a guinea or two, are permanently lost, it is impossible to estimate. If Mrs. Leverson had written for money, she might have kept a record of her publications; what was important to her, like the letters and telegrams from Wilde, she carefully preserved. But, as Mrs. Wyndham says, "she was not a literary careerist, and wrote for the sheer pleasure of seeing herself in print . . . ."[5]

## I *Black and White*

Whether or not her very first publications were those in *Black and White,* they offer an interesting portent of the way in which her career was to develop. In this weekly, Mrs. Leverson published three short stories—"Claude's Aunt," "Mimosa," and "In the Change of Years"[6]—and a series of twenty-four "Letters of Silvia and Aurelia."[7] The first of the three short stories is a comedy; the second, a tragedy; the third, primarily comedy but with serious overtones.

"Claude's Aunt," if it were a Restoration comedy (and it only lacks earthiness to be one), could have the subtitle: "The Marriage Maneuver." When Claude Ferguson visits the country house of his aunt Gladys, he falls in love—as in innumerable rites of initiation in novels and plays and movies, largely French—with an older woman, Mrs. Vervaine, a professional flirt who is estranged from her husband. Claude's aunt, wishing to acquire Claude for her stepdaughter Lucy, who is Claude's own young age, arranges for the unexpected arrival of Colonel Gray, Mrs. Vervaine's lover, and for Claude, "by accident," to witness the loving reunion between Colonel Gray and Mrs. Vervaine. When the strategem succeeds, Claude transfers his affections to Lucy. Another situation, earlier in the story, which is also lifted from familiar stage devices, is the discovery by Lucy of a love letter written by Claude to Mrs. Vervaine.

Other characters include a young married couple, Arthur and Sylvia, whose newlywed bliss adds to the atmosphere of matchmaking and marriage; Mr. Thorne, a bachelor; and Mr. Vincent, an 1890's dandy. Vincent, in his bossy elegance, is an amusing figure; with him, Mrs. Leverson's preoccupation with boutonnieres begins to be evident: Vincent has "prize carnations . . . sent down from town in a cardboard box, twice daily. . . . " The characters have only one, two, or three traits, never more: Claude is emotional, impetuous, and romantic, in a word, young; Lucy, the same; Mrs. Vervaine, sly and flirtatious; Gladys, Claude's aunt, shrewd; Colonel Gray, no traits at all. Mrs. Vervaine has tired "Japanese" looks that foreshadow the Japanese-looking lady Mrs. Raymond in *Love's Shadow,* whom Cecil Reeve loves and whom Lord Selsey, Cecil's uncle, marries. Certainly the characters in "Claude's Aunt"—the title is probably an echo of *Charley's Aunt*[8] —are as flat as Oscar Wilde's. When one of the flattest, Colonel Gray, appears on the scene, we read: "Gladys rose to greet a man of fifty, who had exactly the appearance that an actor would 'make up' for a conventional middle-aged cavalry officer."

"Claude's Aunt" shows that Mrs. Leverson was a humorist from the beginning, and the quick pace and the brevity of the paragraphs reveal that, whatever she had earlier written or published, she was already accustomed to a short, snappy type of journalistic paragraph; and, more important, her instinctive turn was for dialogue. The dialogue is theatrical in nature, and the story is arranged in a series of conversational exchanges, like a play with many short scenes; it is divided into parts—they could be called acts—like a play. The story reads like a scenario, and there is a climactic ball scene, as there is in everything from *The Cherry Orchard* to *My Fair Lady.* Was it Wilde's influence or her own natural bent that led her to a quasi-dramatic form?

The dialogue of "Claude's Aunt" is lively, if not brilliant, and an occasional remark already has the authentic Leverson ring: "Mr. and Mrs. Ferguson [Claude's parents] were very pleased with the letters they received from Claude, though they were shorter than his telegrams and less numerous." "Claude's Aunt" is a workmanlike trifle, which could have been made into a trifling and probably charming play; but Mrs. Leverson, as we shall see in Chapter 4, attempted only one play for production—"The Triflers"—which was never finished.

"Mimosa," Mrs. Leverson's second story, is a tragedy more in intention than in effect. It is most uncharacteristic, in that only a certain dry restraint keeps it from mawkishness. In this simple story about a young country girl with the appropriate country name of Annie Croft, and with the pet name of Mimosa, given to her by the young artist Cecil Thorpe, who comes to stay at her father's farm, Mrs. Leverson aims at sentiment and at romance. Cecil paints Mimosa's portrait and declares his love for her, which the naïve girl ardently returns. When Cecil leaves, Mimosa is as innocent as he had found her, and he promises to return. When he does return, he is too late; he arrives just on the eve of her marriage to the neighboring young farmer—who is, of course, named "John." During Cecil's absence he had achieved success and fame with his portrait of Mimosa, but Mimosa herself gradually came to despair of his return. On her wedding day, after the ceremony—Cecil has left her, this time irrevocably, on learning of her marriage—she is close to taking poison. But "then the influence of the simple religion, in which she had been brought up, asserted itself . . .," she joins her new husband, and the story ends. Religion, which hardly ever appears in Mrs. Leverson's writings, has an operative if unconvincing role in this story.

If this simple tale were more Wordsworthian or more allegorized, it might achieve the pathos at which it aims. The theme may concern the selfishness of art; for, when Cecil returns to Mimosa, he has realized that her portrait is the best thing he has ever done, and he tells her," my *art* is really dependent on *you.*" Moreover, though he loves her, he loves his painting, or himself, more. In contrast to Mimosa's deep, unselfish love, Cecil's is shared with another mistress, his painting; and his love for Mimosa and his art is shallow, since he can barely be troubled to write a letter to her and since, as he well knows, he is not a very good painter.

The impression the story makes is that of a step taken in the wrong direction. There is a clear narrative line, but the anecdote is hackneyed. The closest to humor the story comes is in a description of Cecil's success: "he was made much of by a section of Society, the feminine members of which are free from all solicitudes except that of looking prettier than their neighbors." Pale, only remotely poignant, "Mimosa" shows Mrs. Leverson as divesting herself of her sense of comedy and thereby as depriving herself of her most attractive talent.

The title of Mrs. Leverson's last *Black and White* story, "In the Change of Years," apparently refers to certain changes wrought by time, particularly the transfer of the heroine's—Alice Herbert's—love of her fiancé, Frederick Langton, to a less pompous suitor, Lance Challoner. The change does not seem much for the better: though Fred is pompous and money-minded, Lance is vain, handsome, and silly. When Alice considers the change in Fred, who has returned after making a fortune in South Africa, her mixture of shallowness, true feeling, and girlishness (she is eighteen) is an interesting one: "He was earnest, poor and had a moustache. It's not the same man I was engaged to, or, perhaps, I am not the same woman? If he shaved his beard, and lost all his money would he be possible again?" When Alice breaks her engagement to Fred, he promptly proposes to another girl, the horsy "modern" Ida Hurst. Alice thinks she has been abandoned by Lance, who has returned to London from the northern seaside village where most of the action takes place; but an inflammation of the lungs has been the cause of his silence. After a sickbed reconciliation, the story ends happily—except for Dormer Ellis.

Dormer is Lance's close friend, with whom he has shared a flat; and Dormer is as sober and conservative a barrister as Lance is frivolous and romantic. When the story ends a month after the marriage of Alice to Lance, the last lines portray Dormer's sadness: "Dormer, upstairs, surrounded by cigars and drinks, was supposed to be struggling with a brief. He looked sad. He knew that he now took the second place in the heart of Lance, who was very dear to him. From the room below came the sound of their young laughter. . . ." Even if the language is trite, its effect is to show that the "change" of the title is also a change in Dormer Ellis' life.

The surprisingly melancholy conclusion of the story just quoted may be consonant with the theme, but it is not with the prevailing tone of the story, which is light. Alice Herbert's mother is the first of those studies of comic dowagers, like Lady Kellynch and Lady Cannon, which enliven the novels. Authors often overdo a first inspiration, which additional practice refines; and Mrs. Herbert, with her neurasthenia, her self-indulgence, and her innocent preoccupation with social trivialities, is coarsely executed in comparison with her descendants in the novels. Lance is a harmless fop with his guitar and warbling of sentimental songs, but we wonder why Alice is in the least interested in him. Alice is like a girlish study of Edith Ottley, heroine of three of the novels, in her sensitivity, interest in the arts, and quiet beauty.

There are two complexly conceived scenes in the story. The first is on a fishing boat expedition where, amid the landing of small fish and the jealous intervention of Ida Hurst, Lance declares his love to Alice. The other is the scene of Alice alone by the sea in the little northern town of Sandby. She has rejected Fred, and Lance has apparently abandoned her:

> The little place was full of memories, and she would sit alone, watching the serene irony of unconscious nature, wondering at the harshness, the cruel, unmeaning futility of life.
>
> Supreme summer was over. The first chill of autumn was in the air. The falling leaves had the poetic grace of fading things. Soon the whole earth would be dying of old age and weariness. Already the frequent showers fell like tears, like bitter tears of resignation to the inevitable approach of winter.
>
> But there is always a feeling of life and hope in the restless movement of the sea.
>
> Alice was watching it one day, as she sat on the beach, while a crude, belated band played a valse. It was a commonplace valse, and one that she associated in her mind with rose-coloured tulle, the scent of stephanotis, small social remarks, and polite struggles for ices and plovers' eggs.

As a whole, the passage fails. It might be suitable for Tolstoy's Anna Karenina, but not for Alice Herbert, whom we barely know. Yet the single-sentence third paragraph is a higher order of cliché than what precedes it, and it tempts us to speculate on what might have been Mrs. Leverson's future as a writer if she had pursued the purely romantic vein. However, the last sentence of all in the quoted passage, with its quick, witty, and close social observation, is an example, and a fine one, of the course she did follow.

"In the Change of Years" is not so satisfactory a story as "Claude's Aunt" because of divided intention; it was only later, in the Edith Ottley novels especially, that Mrs. Leverson could blend comedy and romantic love convincingly. These three short stories have been discussed together because of the contrasts they provide, but the series of twenty-four "Letters of Silvia and Aurelia," written from August 5, 1893, to January 27, 1894, follow the first two short stories and precede—except for the last three letters, which are later—the third story.[9]

## II *The Letters*

These letters, which also appeared in *Black and White*, are an example of a common genre during the period, and Mrs. Leverson's do not differ except in their superior wit and intelligence from other such series in popular periodicals of the1890's. Though Silvia is a country girl in correspondence with her city friend Aurelia—note the names—the tone of the two young women is nearly interchangeable; in both cases it is a lively compound of worldliness, irony, malice, and joking. Aurelia, given her superior position in the city, can assume a harder and more sophisticated pose than Silvia; but Silvia is not a rustic innocent. They gossip about fashion, fads, recipes, their admirers, even their husbands. There is much chitchat about entertaining and domestic problems; the letters, each of which is several hundred words in length and amusingly illustrated, are often highly topical, with references to photography, electric lighting, first nights, and "green carnation tinted paper." Some are funnier than others, but all reveal an easy journalistic skill. One of the most humorous is Letter No. 20,[10] which Mrs. Wyndham quotes; Letter No. 22, from Silvia to Aurelia, is also full of jokes and typical of the series:

> By-the-way, I must answer that remark of yours—meant, I know, most kindly—about *culture* not being *smart*. Oh, Aurelia! as if I didn't know that! No one could possibly listen to the conversation in your pretty drawing-room, darling, without observing how fashionable it is to be quite ignorant and rather brainless. The last time I dined with you I heard these three remarks—the first from a gushing middle-aged lady:—
>
> "It's the dream of my life to go to Venice. Fancy floating about in a lagoon! And the Viennese are *so* charming, too, I believe!"

A pretty girl exclaimed: "Oh yes, the 'Heavenly Twins'—I *must* get it—I *love* dear George Eliot."

And a young man said, quite seriously: "An Ibsenite? No—I'm in the Army."

In the same letter, Silvia has sent a "Mr. Newman Haye" a hand-worked letter case as a Christmas gift, and he responds: "We can forgive a person for making a useful thing as long as he does not admire it. The only excuse for making a useless thing is that one admires it intensely." Mrs. Leverson had already used the last epigram in one of her Wilde parodies in *Punch*, on July 15, 1893; and we wonder if Wilde himself had originated the remark.

The light satire of the twenty-four letters makes pleasant reading today. Their easy humor, particularly the predilection for jokes of the type already quoted, is echoed here and there in the novels written fifteen or twenty years later.

Mrs. Leverson's next series of letters of the Silvia-Aurelia type is much more entertaining. The reasons may be that she was now confident of her individual tone and that she was writing for *Punch*, a leading periodical throughout most of the nineteenth century and perhaps the most famous humorous magazine that has ever existed. Many of *Punch*'s jokes of this era—though not Mrs. Leverson's—today seem wordy and emphatic, and its chief interest for us is in the animated guide it provides to the manners and mores of the time.

Mrs. Leverson's contributions to *Punch* are extremely topical. The series of letters beginning on May 26, 1894, and ending December 12, 1896, are a picture of London and country-house society as full of detail as a nineteenth-century genre painting by William Frith. The correspondents are Marjorie and Gladys: there are eight "Letters to [or from] a Débutante," four "Letters to [or from] a Fiancée," and two "Letters of Marjorie and Gladys."[11] The "Débutante" is Gladys, and the letters trace her romantic flings during her first year or two—with Oriel Crampton, just down from Oxford and devoted to good works and stamp collecting; with Captain Mashington, who is poor but waltzes beautifully; with Heinrich Kleingelder, who gives huge dinner parties at the Savoy and plays a bassoon ("*but very little, and only in private*") and one or two others. Gladys' entry into society is encouraged and guided by Marjorie, who comments on Gladys' career with horror, joy, and malice and who gives much cynical good advice. The first letter from Marjorie to Gladys is perhaps the best of all; in it, Marjorie advises:

You say you are rather at a loss for the small change of conversation, and you want to know (for instance) what to say to an Author whose books you have not read, an Artist whose pictures you have not seen, a Composer, or an Explorer, of whom you have never heard.

Generalise. Be cautious. Do not plunge hastily into some rash assumption which you may afterwards regret—a recklessness that leads to such dangers as that of telling Mr. Whistler that "*Bubbles*" is your favourite of his pictures, or of congratulating Mr. Oscar Wilde on the success of "*Dodo*." Say, vaguely, "I am *so* interested in your work, Mr. So-and-So," and leave *him* to give information about it. . . .

When you meet a writer, and you are not sure whether he is the author of a burlesque, or of serious articles for an important review, a safe general remark for a young girl is, "I am *so* afraid of you, Mr. So-and-So; I hear you are so dreadfully clever!" This is one of those unanswerable speeches that for the moment may cast a slight gloom over the conversation, but Mr. So-and-So will presently revive, and it is just possible that you may find out from his remarks whether he is funny or serious. If you do not, it does not matter. . . .

If you meet the sort of person (you will) who says that all he cares about is to bathe his head in God's beautiful sunlight, you may tell him that you are very highly strung, and "neurasthenic." He will probably lend you LeGallienne's Poems, and tell people you are quite charming. . . .

If you are asked what you think about ladies smoking, say it all depends where, how, and when they do it; thus implying you would not like to see a lady smoking a short pipe in the park on Sunday morning. But, under certain circumstances, you may *occasionally* have your *first* cigarette. You need not cough, but laugh a good deal. (Letter of May 26, 1894)

When Gladys is about to begin her second season, Marjorie sends her some "definitions" from a dictionary she is compiling for Gladys's use:

*Art*. A subject of discussion; mild at tea-time, often heated after dinner. [*Note.*—Do not take sides. Mention that Whistler has a picture in the Luxembourg, or say—with a smile or not, as the occasion may suggest—that Sir Frederic is the President of the Academy.]

*Beauty*. An expensive luxury.

*Boy.* If "dear," any effective man under forty. If "horrid," about twelve, and to be propitiated with nuts, knives, and ships. [*Note.*—Do not offend him.]

*Blasphemy.* Any discussion on religion. [*Note.*—Look shocked, but not bored.]

*Coquetry.* A manner sometimes assumed by elderly ladies and very young gentlemen.

*Cynicism.* Truthfulness.

*Eccentricity.* Talent.

*Foreigners.* Often decorative; generally dangerous.

*Friendship.* The mutual dislike of people on intimate terms. Or, a euphuism for love.

*Failure.* An entertainment to which one has not been invited.

*Goodness.* The conduct of one's mother.

*Nature.* It has gone out of fashion, except in novels you must not say you have read.

*Sincerity.* Rudeness.

*Ugliness.* Rather fashionable.

*Zoological Gardens.* Of course not. Nobody goes there now. Besides, you never know whom you may meet. (Letter of January 26, 1895)

Mrs. Leverson was fascinated with the figure of the 1890's esthete—undoubtedly in part because of her friendship with Wilde, the greatest exemplar of the type—and Gladys, in her adventures in society, meets several: Mr. De Verney, to whom she is attracted because she has heard he takes cocaine but whom she rejects because he is "too thin and too fond of jewellery" (Letter of November 28, 1896); Baby Beaumont, who is "really almost nineteen, but wonderfully well preserved, very clever, and so cynical that he is quite an optimist" and who "is always changing his clothes, has two button-holes sent down from London daily . . . he 'intends to revive the gardenia' " (Letter of October 6, 1894); and "Cissy" Cashmore, who is heard to say to his valet, "Take away that eau-de-cologne—it's corked" (Letter of October 27, 1894)—a remark that Mrs. Leverson was to use again for "Cissy" Carington, the esthete of "The Quest of Sorrow" in the *Yellow Book.* Cissy wears "a huge green carnation"; Baby writes letters to seventeen periodicals "denying he had written *The Mauve Camellia";* and "Archie Weirdsley" (Aubrey Beardsley) is mentioned (*Punch* also calls him "Mortarthurio Whiskersley," "Daubaway Weirdsley," and so on, and printed many caricatures of his drawings during the 1890's). In Mrs. Leverson's writings this type of esthete survived Wilde's downfall in early 1895; for Mrs. Leverson—though she no longer mentions Wilde—is still using the esthete as a subject for camp satire in the letters of late 1895 and 1896.

## III *Parodies*

Her keen sense of the ridiculous is also shown in the numerous parodies and lampoons she wrote for *Punch* in the mid-1890's. There are four of Wilde, three of Max Beerbohm, several of various other authors.[12] Naturally, the Wilde parodies deserve attention first. The sketches that appeared in *Punch* from 1893 to 1895 (as has been noted in Chapter 1) were inspired by *The Picture of Dorian Gray, The Sphinx, An Ideal Husband,* and *The Importance of Being Earnest.*

The first of these parodies of Wilde's style is the best. Called "An Afternoon Party,"[13] it is a lively and quarrelsome dialogue among a highly assorted group of contemporary "celebrities," including Charley's Aunt,[14] Madame Santuzza (the heroine of *Cavalleria Rusticana*), Mrs. Tanqueray, Nora (of *Doll's House*), Lady Windermere, and Princess Salome; gentlemen include a Captain Coddington, Lord Henry Wotton, and Lord Illingworth. The conversation is a disconnected succession of jokes, puns, and Wilde-like pseudo-epigrams, such as Lord Illingworth's "Valour is the better part of indiscretion." Princess Salome is amusing parody whether or not one is acquainted with Wilde in his pretentiously lyric vein: " 'Is that mayonnaise?' asked the Princess Salome of Captain Coddington, who had taken her to the buffet. 'I think it is mayonnaise. I am sure it is mayonnaise. It is mayonnaise of salmon, pink as a branch of coral which fishermen find in the twilight of the sea, and which they keep for the King. It is pinker than the pink roses that bloom in the Queen's garden. The pink roses that bloom in the garden of the Queen of Arabia are not so pink.' "

In the following year, 1894, appeared "The Minx—a Poem in Prose,"[15] which is in the form of an interview of the Egyptian Sphinx by a Poet. The Sphinx, rather a prima donna, reviews events and personalities of Egyptian history in a casual, *haut-monde* sort of way. Wilde's poem *The Sphinx* had been published earlier in this year; and he wrote to the Sphinx, as he now called her: "I delight in your literary 'minx.' It is most brilliant, but should be longer; we want more of it."[16]

The other two parodies of Wilde are even shorter than "The Minx." The first is called "Overheard Fragment of a Dialogue"[17] and consists of a conversation between Lord Goring and Lord Illingworth which mocks both the epigrammatic Wilde ("If one tells the truth, one is sure sooner or later to be found out") and the lyric Wilde ("The sky is like a hard hollow sapphire"). The second is called "The Advisability of Not Being Brought up in a Handbag: A Trivial Tragedy for Wonderful People":[18] the title of this satire on *The Importance of Being Earnest* is almost as long as the little dialogue that follows it, and that includes such remarks as, from a character named Algy, "It is such a blessing, Aunt Augusta, that a woman always grows exactly like her aunt. It is such a curse that a man never grows exactly like his uncle. It is the greatest tragedy of modern life." Wilde's last premiere was *The Importance of Being Earnest*, which had taken place earlier, on February 14, 1895, and his arrest and trials beginning a few weeks later ended both him and the Sphinx's parodies of his successes.

Max Beerbohm had known Mrs. Leverson even longer than Wilde; for, as Mrs. Wyndham writes, "Max Beerbohm and Ada had been close friends ever since she saw him first at a dancing class—she nearly grown-up and he a little boy in a sailor-suit. She would often tell of how sweet he looked when holding out his white trousers in an attempt to curtsey. . . . Max fell in love with Ada while he was at Oxford; in a letter he compared her mouth to a 'little red boat with white sailors in it.' "[19] Mrs. Leverson was also a friend of Max's mother; of his two sisters, Constance and Agnes; and of his half-brother, Beerbohm Tree. Max was a frequent guest in her various London residences, and in later years on her Italian expeditions she visited him in Rapallo.

Max became famous with his flippant history of George IV and with his defense of cosmetics in the first number of the *Yellow Book*. Mrs. Leverson's "A Phalse Note on George the Fourth (*A Brown Study in a Yellow Book*)"[20] takes Max's habit of coining words ("bauble-tit" and "pop-limbo") and of using convoluted and archaic phrases and heightens them to absurdity: "Queen Caroline was a mimsy, outmoded woman, a sly serio, who gadded hither and thither shrieking for the unbecoming. Mrs. Phox ensorcelled George with her beautiful, silly phace, shadowed with vermeil tinct and trimly pencilled. There was no secernment between her soul and surface; she was mere, *insouciant*, with a rare dulcedo." The proportion of nonsense is higher than in Joyce's parodies in the "Oxen of the Sun" episode in *Ulysses*, yet Mrs. Leverson's little essay is not dissimilar.

Early in the following year Mrs. Leverson published "A Few Words with Mr. Max Beerbohm," an interview with Max which, though it appeared in the *Sketch* and not in *Punch*, should be considered here.[21] Like a good reporter, Mrs. Leverson describes Max's appearance (and includes his photograph as a small boy in a sailor suit) and leads him to talk about his background and education, his current fame, and his plans for the future. Her technique as an interviewer is too unobtrusive for anything of herself to emerge, but her love of jokes is shown by the end of her piece, when Max claims that he is "writing a treatise upon 'The Brothers of Great Men,' including a series of psychological sketches of Mr. Willie Wilde, Mr. Austen Chamberlain, and others." Mrs. Leverson enquires, "You are a brother of Mr. Beerbohm Tree, I believe?"; Max answers, "Yes; he is coming into the series!"

To return to *Punch*, Mrs. Leverson's other two pieces on Max are Part I of "From the Queer and Yellow Book"—signed "Max Mereboom"—and a little poem, signed the same way, "Be It Cosiness."[22] The first pretends that Max, as historian, is looking back upon the year 1894 from some point in the future and describing the customs and celebrities of that period. *The Mauve Camellia* once again appears; and so do dining at the Savoy, *Charley's Aunt*, the Decadents, "Aubrey Weirdsley," and so forth. The sketch affects the mood of Samuel Pepys or John Evelyn, with additions of Max's peculiar vocabulary—"implected," "mobled," and the like. The final bit of Beerbohmiana, "Be It Cosiness," is a jaunty little jingle about Max's retirement to the country:

With gibe and jest, I wrote my best,
On leaving Alma Mater,
In language quaint defended paint,
And now disparage Pater.

King George I chaffed, and lightly laughed
At 1880 crazes,
In dainty prose I wrote of hose
And sang a dandy's praises.

Now London gay I leave for aye,
A villa I've been buying,
A life-long lease—to live in peace
The life for which I'm sighing.

Not prince nor Czar, nor Shah-Zada
(Though gaudy be his turban),
Nor Royal boy can know the joy
Of cosiness suburban!

All day the news I'll read, and muse
Of all that was and will be;
If bored I feel, to town I'll steal,
Once more to witness *Trilby*.

Mrs. Leverson wrote very few poems. Two others, both parodies—"Foam-Flowers" and "Intention"—are discussed later.

Of the few other miscellaneous contributions to *Punch,* the first is two letters to the editor of *Punch* about love.[23] One is from "A Sensible Pessimist" who asserts the impossibility of finding a wife because a man must ask himself, of any female prospect,

"Will she make me a good wife? Can she clean chimneys, cook and mend; is she capable of discussing intellectually subjects of interest—such as dentistry, hunting, symbolism, and so forth—with her husband? Can she grind the organ, play the comb, is she active at crossing-sweeping and cradle-rocking, quick at smiling away one's smiles and frowning away one's tears, ready to greet all my friends with the same amiability she shows to *me,* is she prepared for intelligent begging-letter-writing, can she scour, skirt-dance, recite, carve, mangle, and fence?" Too often he is bound to answer, "No, she cannot; so what good is she to me?"

In the other letter, signed "Happy Brown Bess," Bess is an aged woman who at the age of seventy-two had made an unfortunate marriage: her husband died from boredom within a few weeks. But Bess still believes in marriage, and she affirms in a muddled way that there are "many . . . pure, gentle, and loving old women, who, I think, would gladly enter matrimony." Both letters are droll catalogues of *idées reçues*.

In "The Plain Tale of Cinderella, Told by Three Authors,"[24] Mrs. Leverson looses gentle barbs of satire at three authors: Kipling, Pearl Craigie, and George Moore.

The nature of parody is, of course, to exaggerate for humorous purposes the salient and unique features of an author's style. With Kipling, Mrs. Leverson emphasizes the terse, "masculine" vigor; with John Oliver Hobbes, a type of ultrasophisticated shallow paradox; with Moore, the graphic and sex-oriented Naturalism.

The first is "R-dy-rd K-pl-ng," and his version of Cinderella begins: "The manner of it was in this way. Understand clearly that there was not a word to be said against Cinderella—not a shadow of a breath. She was good and lovely, with green eyes under eyebrows as black and as straight as the borders of the *Indian Gazette* when a big man dies. But——— Well, her step-sisters were jealous of her. Which is curious." The second parody is signed "J-hn Ol-v-r H-bbs." The correct spelling is "Hobbes," and it is a penname for Mrs. Pearl Craigie, a popular novelist of the period and a friend and collaborator of George Moore's. We cite part of the description of Cinderella: "To look at her was to think of a scaffolding. Hair dishonestly golden, sparkling with peroxide and insincerity, framed a face of such extraordinary beauty that to behold it was to doubt the genuineness of the creation."

The title of the third parody—"Cinderella Waters"—alludes to "G-rge M—re's" celebrated novel of 1894, *Esther Waters.* Mrs. Leverson's version ends: "With a sigh, she tried not to think of the glare and rustle of silk, of waltz tunes. She rose and began slowly ironing out some ragged dusters. . . . Then she started and her flesh burnt, for the red-hot flat-iron that she had accidentally dropped on her foot seemed to her like a message from a lover. . . ."

The last contribution to *Punch,* "In a Boudoir,"[25] is one of the longest, a two-page dialogue between two young women. Blanche is "fair and irresponsible"; Enid, "dark and sensible." Both are married, but Blanche has admirers, including a Mr. Lance Challoner: Mrs. Leverson borrowed his name from her own *Black and White* story, "In the Change of Years." Lance arrives to pay court, preceded by Blanche's sixteen-year-old brother Savile, who has wanted to marry a music-hall artiste, aged forty and the mother of six, but who now announces that he has broken off with her. He is a prototype of the sixteen-year-old Savile in *The Twelfth Hour,* who is also unsuccessfully in love, in his case with the elderly diva, Adelina Patti. The dialogue is intended to oppose the flirtatious affectations of Blanche to the common sense of Enid, but Blanche is neither sufficiently silly nor Enid sufficiently firm for the contrast to be very effective. "In a Boudoir" has its interest as a picture of fashionable young women's conversation, but it is not one of Mrs. Leverson's stronger efforts. Her best pieces for *Punch* are probably the Débutante Letters and the first parody of Wilde.

## IV *The Yellow Book*

As we noted earlier, the distinction of Mrs. Leverson's position in the literary life of the 1890's is indicated by her having been asked to contribute to the *Yellow Book* and by a reproduction of her portrait by Walter Sickert in the same issue in which the first of her two stories appeared.[26] Her position may be attributed as much to her salon and to her friendships with artists and writers as to her own literary efforts up to that time, clever and original though these may often have been. Her two stories—"Suggestion" and "The Quest of Sorrow"[27]—are particularly suited to the *Yellow Book* as an organ of the Decadent movement because each is a study of a young Decadent. Her own attitude toward the movement and toward her two young heroes is highly observant and amused but altogether detached. Her affectionate, even loving, interest in her friends among the movement never cost her her objectivity. The use of the first-person angle of narration in both stories is the main device behind which her own opinions shelter. We do not imply, however, that the stories are not sharply satirical, nor that no norm of common sense, and even of morality, transpires. Her judgments are imposed the more firmly by the air of rational detachment and of good humor, but we must guess at or assume them by certain ironic edges, never by open statement.

The chief character of "Suggestion" is Cecil ("Cissy") Carington, who has defeated his widowed father's prospective marriage to a respectable matron because she had spoken of him as "that intolerable, effeminate boy." Instead, he arranges his father's marriage with a sensitive and beautiful girl of twenty, Laura Egerton. The marriage quickly disillusions both partners; Mr. Carington returns to his mistress, who lives in a small house opposite the Brompton Oratory; and Cecil, after his one and only pang of conscience, arranges a love affair between his young stepmother and another esthete, Adrian Grant. As a study in cold self-indulgence and monolithic vanity, Cecil is frightening. He even praises his own good looks by praising his mother's:

> Every one says I am strangely like my mother. Her face was of that pure and perfect oval one so seldom sees, with delicate features, rose-bud mouth, and soft flaxen hair. A blondness without insipidity, for the dark-blue eyes are fringed with dark lashes, and from their languorous depths looks out a soft mockery. I have a curious ideal devotion to my mother; she died when I was quite young—only two months old—and I often spend hours thinking of her, as I gaze at myself in the mirror.

Cecil has numerous classic homosexual traits, with his mother fixation, his narcissism, his antagonism to his father, his feminine slyness, his obsessive neurasthenia, and his love of posturing and posing. His tastes are a compendium of the esthete's foibles, whether it be his preference for Pierre Loti and lilies of the valley for his buttonhole, or his wish to have "an onyx-paved bath-room, with soft apricot-coloured light shimmering through the blue-lined green curtains in my chambers. . . ." Cecil would be intolerable if it were not for his own, and his creator's, wit: he says that Adrian Grant "has a little money of his own—enough for his telegrams, but not enough for his buttonholes . . ."; at dinner with Adrian, he "can not help hoping . . . that the shaded candles were staining to a richer rose the waking wonder of my face"; Adrian's "gorgeous" studio is, he says, at once like "the calm retreat of a mediaeval saint and the luxurious abode of a modern Pagan. One feels that everything could be done there, everything from praying to flirting—everything except painting." "Suggestions" is a skillful character study of rich period interest, in that the parody of the esthete's life style is more cunning than earlier parodies. And the story is rich enough for our reactions to be complex; we can despise and pity and deplore and find sympathetic young Cecil and his intrigues. He is the first full character that Mrs. Leverson created.

"The Quest of Sorrow" is neither quite so amusing nor so suggestive as "Suggestion." Since its hero is Cecil Carington a few years older, we wonder if Mrs. Leverson had planned these two short stories as the first two chapters of a novel. In "Suggestion" Cecil's problem was to defeat his father; in "The Quest of Sorrow," he has discovered that he has never experienced defeat or failure of any kind and determines, perversely enough, to seek out and achieve "sorrow." His quest is like a debased version of Keats's search for beauty in "Ode on Melancholy."

First, Cecil hopes to be disappointed by failure in the publication of a poem, which he calls "Foam-Flowers." (He signs the poem—"as my things are always signed—'Lys de la Vallée.' ") This poem in close-to-sonnet form is supercharged with a Romanticism in which hyacinths are gold, not blue; poppies are white, not red; and "a bird sings . . . amid the mad Mimosa's scented spray. . . ." But the desired disappointment does not result, since an editor accepts "Foam-Flowers" as an "amusing parody on a certain modern school of verse."

Cecil now becomes pure cad and decides to fall hopelessly in love with the fiancée, Alice Sinclair, of his good friend Freddy, since his frustration in this quest will certainly lead to sorrow. But his strategems, at an ice-skating rink and elsewhere, succeed to the extent that Alice decides to abandon Freddy for him. The shock of success is too much for Cecil, and he rejects Alice's offer. Alice marries Freddy, and Cecil resigns himself to a life of joy, barren of sadness and its recondite rewards.

The story has, as does "Suggestion," its serious subject, which becomes evident on examination. Cecil is a study in the complete hedonist, and we see in his artful attitudes an ironic reduction of some of Wilde's preachments and even of Walter Pater's before him. Mrs. Leverson's morality is subtle enough that we do not condemn Cecil on first reading; perfect egotism, whether of Richard III or of anyone else, is as engaging as anything perfect always is, at least when coupled with wit: "we had gone to skate at that absurd modern place where the ice is as artificial as the people, and more polished"; "So I wrote a poem. It was beautiful, but that I couldn't help"; "Yes, exile. For to-morrow I leave England. To-morrow I go to bury myself in some remote spot—perhaps to Trouville. . . ."

Because the second Cecil is older than the first, he is both less appealing and less appalling, but the two short stories are alike in their quiet condemnation of a way of life that is heartless in its wit and selfish in its elegance. We cannot generalize and assume that they represent Mrs. Leverson's judgment of the 1890's; for, after all, the stories make their primary effect as comedies. The stories are, however, too assured in manner for us to suspect some kind of insecurity of intention on Mrs. Leverson's part. She was flexible enough, and large enough, not to deplore; her comic spirit could encompass a great deal that she knew was flimsy and false. The *Yellow Book* is a central document of the 1890's; and Mrs. Leverson's two stories, in their perception and shrewdness, are an important contribution to its authenticity.

## CHAPTER 4

# *Minor Works, 1903–1930*

THERE is no evidence in the years just at the turn of the twentieth century of any publications by Mrs. Leverson, a lacuna in her career that is hard to explain. There may have been several causes. As someone has observed, the nature of a Sphinx is to be silent, but, more to the point, it may have been that her responsibilities as a wife and mother occupied more of her time; certainly the downhill path of her marriage, soon to end in separation and her husband's removal to Canada, accelerated at this time. Perhaps she wrote short pieces all trace of which has been lost; perhaps she began works that she did not complete: there is evidence in her later life of works started but never finished, such as a biography of Robert Ross and a seventh novel.[1] Still another explanation is that the trial and exile of Wilde and his death in 1900 may have inhibited her creativity; he, if anyone, had inspired her career, and with him gone, her career came to a temporary halt.

### I *The Unfinished Play*

Another unfinished project that could have occupied her writing hours at this time, if she did not altogether cease writing, was her play with the attractive title of "The Triflers." Mrs. Wyndham says that her mother worked on the play for many years:

> Of all the galaxy of talent, and it was a period rich in glamorous theatrical figures, the Sphinx's favourite actor was Charles Hawtrey. He was neither good-looking nor romantic. Yet the naturalistic manner of his acting illuminated everything he did on the stage. It was her dream to write a play for him. Seeing one in Paris which she thought would be easy to adapt for the English stage, Ada persuaded Ernest to buy the dramatic rights. It satirised a shallow, cynical, frivolous group of people who were supposed to behave as they did because

they were living at the Fin de Siècle. . . . She ignored the dialogue of the French original and wrote her own. The play was altered very slightly, again and again. In the first version there was a Duchess and a conservatory, as in the plays of Wilde. One scene satirises the pose of morbidity adopted by some at that time. In a conversation between a young married woman and her lover, she pretends to believe that double suicide is the only solution to all true love problems, and is always urging him towards this end; he is bored and complains that he has not got the time, also that he would have to resign from his Club, the Marlborough, were he to do what she asks. . . .

. . . The plot, although slight, is ingenious. The last version was made in the late Twenties for the ageing Mrs. Patrick Campbell. By that time, the Duchess and the conservatory had been dropped, and taxis, telephones, and mentions of the Sitwells and Noel Coward had been added. The play was never quite finished and Ada failed to achieve her ambition to hear her word spoken on the stage by Charles Hawtrey, or indeed by any one else.[2]

## II *The* Referee

The outburst of productivity that followed this silent interval took the form of a weekly column for a periodical called the *Referee*, from June 28, 1903, to August 20, 1905—113 columns,[3] averaging 1,350 words each: a total of over 150,000 words, or the length of two average-sized novels in a space of a little over two years. The format of the *Referee* seems quaint today; it cost one penny, and it covered events of the theater, music, business, turf, and other news. The contributors signed themselves in Arthurian manner—Lancelot, Merlin, Tristram, and so on. Mrs. Leverson, who signed herself "Elaine," called her column "White and Gold"; it appeared usually on page 7, sometimes on page 9.

Because the amount of weekly wordage was so large, Mrs. Leverson's style is thinner in these columns. It is amiable and precise and, in contrast to other columns of the same nature in contemporary periodicals, more reserved or restrained. It is devoid of the sentimentality, sensationalism, and gush typical of ladies' columns before and since, but it seldom rises to those moments of high absurdity that, for example, her *Punch* parodies attain. Her material is easy reading; it does not seem dated, as, considering the topicality of its subjects, it might well have; but hers is more a conscientious and clever performance than an inspired one.

Her subjects are manifold, and they are oriented toward the *Referee's* women readers. They include food, servants, the servant problem, gift-giving, literary figures, dieting, fortune-telling (both cards and palmistry), fans, first nights, dandies, children's toys, children's parties, love, flirtation, snobs, dinner table decorations, motoring, superstitions, etiquette, hair styles. Mrs. Leverson comments frequently on oddities in the American scene, but her tone is pleasantly pro-American, and her admiration for France and everything French is often expressed. Probably one-third of her material deals with women's fashions, and here her restraint serves her well; she was incapable of affecting either the mad breathlessness of *Vogue* or the hearty "sensible" Lois Long approach to fashion.

We learn much about Mrs. Leverson herself from "White and Gold"—not only of her love for France, but also her love of London: "Where in Europe can be found a metropolis so interesting, so sympathetic, and so delightful? But I am an irretrievable Cockney!" (June 19, 1904). Her favorite flower was the gardenia (August 23, 1903). She believed that marriage was to a woman's advantage, seldom if ever to a man's (March 6, 1904); and, most candidly, "The only thing that one can fairly rely on in married life is character" (February 14, 1904)—which might be the motto for her three Ottley novels or, in fact, for her own marriage.

Literature is not often discussed, though she speaks of her admiration for Henry James (February 21, 1904) and William Dean Howells (April 17, 1904). Shaw—"that brilliant vegetarian"—amused more than educated her, and she wrote one quite funny column (July 9, 1905) about her discovery that Shaw's objection to women's wearing of furs and feathers was not his love for animals and birds but was, instead, envy:

> After condemning the bad taste of a lady who sat in front of him in a stall at the opera wearing the corpse of a large white bird stuck over one ear, one discovers that the motive of his protest and the crux of his complaint lies in the fact that he is not allowed to do the same. "If I," he says, with a touch of real bitterness, "had presented myself at the doors with a grouse in my hair, I should have been refused admission." Doubtless this is only too true. Perhaps it is hard. Mr. Shaw would (I think) look extremely nice with a grouse in his hair, or with vine leaves, or in an ostrich feather boa and a chiffon cloak.

But who would have believed that he could care about wearing these things?

Her sense of humor is never long absent. In one column she considers a new method of teaching parrots to talk by means of a phonograph, which could "repeat into the ears of the birds such sentences as are to be learnt, suitable to their social station"; and then she suggests that the same method should be applied to people (October 4, 1903). Elsewhere she remarks airily, "I believe to a certain extent in palmistry; but not in palmists . . ." (November 22, 1903) and that, though foreign servants are often superior, "A butler in an English household should, however, be English, and as much like an archbishop as possible" (October 11, 1903). She quotes schoolboy boners: "Americans are put to death by elocution" and "Enoch was a man who wrote fables, and sold his birthday for a glass of potash" (December 20, 1903). The word "smart" arouses her to energetic protest:

> . . . Today nearly everybody and everything is described by this epithet, which has lost its meaning. A bride is smart. A hat is smart. So is a wedding, a journal, or a play. The torpedoing of a battleship is described in the same way. We read of "smart" new babies. Before long we shall be confronted in our papers with "The smartest deceases of the past week included . . ." Smart now means fashionable, a word Anthony Trollope drove to death—indeed, it was on its last legs when Mrs. Gore's "Tales of Fashionable Life" ceased to be read. Surely we have driven "smart" to death. Let it be buried (of course smartly). . . . (May 27, 1904)

With the end of her weekly columns for the *Referee* on August 20, 1905, Mrs. Leverson took the major step in her career; she began to write her first novel, *The Twelfth Hour,* which was published two years later in 1907.[4] The columns themselves were a proof of her ability at sustained literary effort, but they must have cramped her creativity; she must often have wished to abandon the format prescribed for a form that imagination itself dictated; to tap deeper, more personal inspirations; to make up her own elegant world rather than to observe and record—no matter with what skill and interest—the plainer world around her. In short, she left journalism for literature. Fiction is in a sense always a protest; even if large elements of the real enter into it, the imagination orders the real into the unreal, into superior clarities, into the generalizations that underlie the flux of specifics. Her work for the *Referee* was no doubt useful preparation for the novels, but it was probably in reaction against the restrictions her column imposed, rather than as a natural outgrowth from it, that she came to write *The Twelfth Hour.*

## III Whom You Should Marry

In 1915, toward the end of her career (1907–16) as a novelist, Mrs. Leverson wrote a five-page introduction to a volume called *Whom You Should Marry;* its subtitle helps to explain the nature of this eccentric book: *Shows the Qualities and Character of Persons Born in Each Month of the Year and Whether, for Instance, a Man Born in May Should Marry a Woman Born in April.* No author is given; he is merely referred to as "an American gentleman." Mrs. Leverson consented to write an introduction either because the book was published by Grant Richards, her own publisher and close friend, who may have hoped that the prestige of her name would enhance sales, or because the subject of the book appealed to her sense of fantasy or nonsense. Like her remark quoted above—"I believe in palmistry to a certain extent, but not in palmists . . ."—Mrs. Leverson was the mixture of skepticism and superstition that most of us are.

Mrs. Leverson begins her introduction by commenting that astrology has been believed by the credulous for thousands of years, and she parodies the very general advice that newspaper astrologers give their readers. But she says she believes that the theory she is now introducing that "one's birth-month affects one's temperament"—which comes from "America, that marvellous country of new inventions, and new religions"—possibly has some validity as "an amiable and amusing fancy." Among the examples she cites from *Whom You Should Marry* are "December-April and November-August are ideal love marriages" and this advice to those born in May: "Guard well your reputation. Control your desire to break up the homes of others." She is particularly interested in the author's remarks about those born in October, her own birth-month: "They possess so many noble traits that it is a crime to permit them to be smothered" and "so many brilliant gifts that they should certainly be brought to life and made a great success of."

Such solemn pronouncements undoubtedly amused Mrs. Leverson. Although she concludes that *Whom You Should Marry* is "well worth quite serious consideration," her remarks hardly support the claim. Her style is complex and graceful; her tone, tolerant, sophisticated, and relaxed. The result is that she only toys with the American gentleman's ideas and thus in effect dismisses them, as well she might have.

## IV *The* English Review

Mrs. Leverson's three little pieces in the *English Review* indicate not only how powerfully the 1890's survived in Mrs. Leverson's mind but how naturally inquisitive she remained about innovations in the arts. Though the 1890's were the touchstone decade to her, she never became conservative in the usual elderly way, for no incrustations of old-fashioned notions impeded her fresh and eager interest in what was new.

"Free Verse" in 1919[5] provides a third example of Mrs. Leverson as poet. The sketch begins with a poem called "Intention," which is a parody of *vers libre*, "by one of the new chaps":

Intention
I.
I think of going to Eastbourne,
I must get some new clothes before I go
To Eastbourne.
I may get a green jumper,
Or some beads,
Or any old thing. . . .
II.
I know the Vicar slightly.
He may be nice to me and call on Sunday.
If he does I shall certainly
Say cheerio to the Blighter. . . .

"Free Verse" is a dialogue about this magnificent poem between Aubrey, an esthete, and his honest uncomprehending friend George:

"*Or some beads!*" he murmured. "Isn't that a perfect line? Don't you see the floridness of frigidity in it, George? DON'T YOU?"

George jumped.

"All right. Don't get excited, old bean. Give me some tea. It's the only real brain stimulant."

Aubrey explains to George that there is a new movement in literature afoot: "There's a man called Eliot. He's great. He counts." And George says knowingly, "Ah, yes. George Eliot. . . ." The dialogue is only two pages long, but the picture it presents of the precious, insistent enthusiast for the new versus the well-meaning, bewildered conservative is complete. As usual, Mrs. Leverson's comic judgment does not permit bias; therefore, Aubrey and George are equally obtuse; and their Molière-like confrontation is dateless in its relevance.

A year later Mrs. Leverson published a longer work in the *English Review*, a short story "The Blow."[6] The story resembles those studies in the *Yellow Book* of the selfish young esthete Cecil Carington of "Suggestion" and "The Quest of Sorrow." The *vita* in *Who's Who* of Stanley Wilson, hero of "The Blow," lists one of his recreations as "wincing." Cecil Carington in the *Yellow Book* had his redeeming rococo qualities, his intelligence, and his devilish malice; but Stanley, though he is like Cecil in his good looks, vanity, and neurasthenia, lacks wit.

The frail anecdote concerns Stanley's desire to break off his relations with Juliet, his Wednesday-afternoon friend. He experiments with farewell letters to her, one of which, surprisingly, contains a line, already mentioned in Chapter 1, from a letter of Wilde's to Mrs. Leverson: "You are one of those—too few, alas!—who are always followed by the flutes of the pagan world. . . ."[7] His letter-writing is interrupted by the arrival of his friend, Captain Eric Yule; Eric is a hearty Englishman, whom Stanley pities for "his possessions, his high spirits, his pink face, and his yellow car." The Captain is in especially high spirits, but Stanley "would not ask the reason for his joy. He feared Eric might tell him." However, when Eric leaves, a letter arrives for Stanley from Juliet, which tersely announces her engagement to Eric ("We are going for our wedding-trip in a caravan on account of petrol"). This "blow" turns the tables, and the story ends with Stanley, in a fit of rage, throwing a bottle of medicine out the window.

Stanley is too mean-spirited to interest us as Cecil Carington does. The story is told in the objective third person; and this distancing, this treating of Stanley like a microscope specimen, keeps us from quite knowing and believing in him, though no epigram is spared by Mrs. Leverson: "Women fell in love with him, but only at first sight . . ." and "He liked books; not novels, but something that made one think. His favourite writer was E. V. Lucas. It was only when he had a temperature that he read Ethel M. Dell." But the most striking inferiority of "The Blow" to the *Yellow Book* stories is probably not the reptilian sluggishness of Stanley but the absence of the 1890's decor in which Cecil moves and of which he is so richly the flower.

Her last piece, in the form of a four-page play, was published in the *English Review* two years later in 1922. Mrs. Leverson was sixty, but "Gentlemen v. Players"[8] shows as sprightly a humor and as appreciative a knowledge of the latest art movements as ever. Aubrey (the gentleman) and George (the cricket player), the same characters met in "Free Verse," reappear, and they have changed little:

> Aubrey (*after a moment*). Have you ever heard of Freud or Jung, George?
> George. Never. And I don't care if I never do. Foreigners are fools.

George is more firmly philistine than he was in "Free Verse," and Aubrey is more rigorously avant-garde; but the opposition between them, and the basic conflict it represents, has not altered. In Aubrey's taste in decoration, he is stridently contemporary ("Decorations by Bakst. Pictures by Wyndham Lewis, Picasso, and Gauguin. Music by Goosens and Stravinsky. Books by Wyndham Lewis, Proust, Stephen Hudson, T. S. Eliot, Osbert Sitwell, and Zola"); but he, or Mrs. Leverson, has preserved a certain taste for the 1890's. Speaking of a new volume of poetry—which George has just called "rot'—Aubrey says,

> In the 'nineties a volume of this kind would have been bound in green leather with gold tooling, and would have consisted chiefly of margin. It might have been all margin; full of beautiful unwritten thoughts. There would have been one limited edition on Japanese paper—five hundred copies for particular friends, six for the general public, and one for America. Now there are poets by the thousand, instead of a small exclusive set. Whether there was ever a golden age

I don't know, but certainly the 'nineties were the dog-days of English poetry. How sultry and exotic they were! . . . But now things seem to me more vivid, more full of colour and spirit than that curious period ever was. . . . The present is what matters. Now. This moment!

In this strange passage, the first half (down to "and one for America") is Mrs. Leverson's memory of a conversation with Oscar Wilde—the first two sentences hers, the third Wilde's—which she repeats in her introduction to *Letters to the Sphinx,* published eight years after "Gentlemen v. Players."[9] Still stranger is the attitude toward the 1890's which Aubrey's statements disclose. "Dog-days" is a term used to describe August, a period of stagnation or inactivity—yet Aubrey adds that they were "sultry and exotic," adjectives of less negative connotation. His claim that the present is "more vivid, more full of colour and spirit" sounds like asseveration. Through Aubrey, Mrs. Leverson seems to be trying both to remember with nostalgia Wilde's wit and the pretty volumes of his day bound in green and gold and to accept at the same time the present—that is, 1922—and acknowledge the revolution in art it was achieving. Yet Aubrey is only a character, not Mrs. Leverson herself; and we must judge his opinions as those of quite a foolish young man. Even the subtitle of "Gentlemen v. Players" (with its pun on Critic: Cricket) is ambiguous: "A Critic Match; With some Conversation about the 'Nineties."

The sketch is also inconclusive in that neither George nor Aubrey is convinced of the other's correctness. George's last remark is, "Do you know, I've seen *The Gondoliers* thirty-one times since the revival?"; and Aubrey replies, "Wonderful how a man can describe himself in one sentence!" Though George and Aubrey have reached their usual impasse, we feel that Mrs. Leverson was meditating on the 1890's, looking back, and reevaluating from the vantage point of the age of Picasso and Stravinsky. The contrast between a book by Wyndham Lewis and "a volume . . . bound in green leather with gold tooling" and consisting "chiefly of margin" is perhaps what "Gentlemen v. Players" is about.

## V. *The* Criterion *and* Letters to the Sphinx

*Letters to the Sphinx,* the tribute to Wilde which ended Mrs. Leverson's literary career is, happily, one of her finest pieces of writing. The volume of her letters from Wilde had long been planned: Robert Ross, who died in 1918, wrote the introduction; and Mrs. Leverson's footnote to it says, "Some years ago, when it was intended to publish this book anonymously, Mr. Robert Ross kindly wrote this prefatory note." What the various reasons for withholding publication were, we do not know—one may have been the wish not to offend various friends still alive who are mentioned in the letters—but it is appropriate that her last published work should concern the friend and mentor who had encouraged her to write so many years before.

Nor is it known when her own reminiscences of Wilde which precede the thirty letters and telegrams were composed. The middle section—"The Last First Night"—was written at least as early as 1925 since it was published in the January, 1926, issue of T. S. Eliot's *Criterion.*[10] The first and third sections—"The Importance of Being Oscar" and "Afterwards"—may also have been written in 1925 or earlier, or at any time within the next five years, since there is no record of their publication before 1930. When Lord Alfred Douglas read *Letters to the Sphinx,* he wrote to Violet Wyndham about her mother: "What an artist she is! In a few lines she has succeeded in creating a perfect impression of Oscar which no one else has ever succeeded in doing. Like Baudelaire she may say: Je sais l'art d'évoquer les minutes heureuses."[11]

In style, the three parts of the essay of reminiscences are of a piece; and the style is at once the most graceful and the most weighty that Mrs. Leverson ever achieved. She turns each ancedote into a little story of its own, with elements artfully spaced and arranged. Her sentences tend to be longer, more complex, more obviously rhythmic, but her habitual one-sentence epigrammatic paragraph, as in the novels, also appears. The tone of unembittered gaiety deepens often into sensitive, graver notes. Even with the intimacy of her portrait, she never says, "It is I who sheltered Wilde"; nor, on the other hand, does she disguise her good deeds and his gratitude for them and his affection. Throughout her writing, her candor is coupled with a fine restraint. Wilde himself so much admired manner and manners (in that order, I think) that he surely would have approved the Sphinx's style in her reminiscences, just as he had lavished praise on her sketches and parodies of the early 1890's.

The volume consists of a brief introduction by Robert Ross

(13–16); an epigram from Swinburne (17)—"Nothing is better, I well think, / Than love; the hidden well-water / Is not so delicate to drink: / This was well seen of me and her"; the three-part Reminiscences (19–49); and the thirty letters and telegrams (50–64). The volume is dedicated "For Raymond" (Raymond Mortimer).

Robert Ross's introduction is, for its length, an elaborate affair. The example we cite below illustrates the nature of his overwriting, with its Sitwellian floridities and sensitivities. And he seems still to be fighting old battles: dutifully, as Wilde's literary executor, he vouches for the genuineness of the thirty letters, but he uses the occasion to deplore the lack of more than two or three "trustworthy" accounts of Wilde, to remark on "the spurious writings and the forged letters attributed to him," and to mention darkly the existence of "enemies." Ross still bore scars from the battles with "Bosie," and one hears in the background, muted through Ross's delicate cadences, all the hullabaloo of Wilde's last years and also the squabbling that took place over his literary remains, the vying of the faithful among themselves for the role of chief mourner, the jealousies and the spite.

Nonetheless, Ross gives the Sphinx full credit. If Robert Sherard's life of Wilde was a "sombre mezzotint," the Sphinx's memoir is an "exquisite pastel." His last paragraph, with its plethora of literary allusions, is Firbankian in its preciosity (minus Firbank's wit), but the tribute to Mrs. Leverson is graceful:

> In writing of one whose egoism was superb it is impossible to be adequate without intruding the first person singular; only through the convention of Willoughby Patterne can we produce a negative of Oscar Wilde, and then the silver print betrays over-exposure. It is impossible to echo even faintly that voice "which conjured wonder out of emptiness." He was indeed a conjurer. To talk with him was to be translated to an enchanted island or to the palaces of the *Fata Morgana*. You could not tell what flowers were at your feet or what fantastic architecture was silhouetted against the purple atmosphere of his conversation. What expert could date the pleasant furniture of his house of life? Who would not kneel in the chapels of that Rimmon? . . . But if Prospero is dead we value all the more the little memories of Miranda.

"Miranda" could have written a good parody of the passage.

What Mrs. Leverson does in "The Importance of Being Oscar" is to set the scene for the rest of the essay by delineating the character of the early 1890's and by showing how Wilde dominated the period. She describes how London in 1894 and 1895 "bloomed out into a sudden flamboyance of taste and of expression. Art, poetry, beauty, dress and decoration became the fashion." She well remembers the enthusiasms of those days—the Overture to *Tannhäuser, Mrs. Tanqueray,* the Gaiety Theatre, the revival of mid-Victorian decoration, Whistler, the de Rezskes. Of Wilde himself, she says, in pungent summary, "The most soft-hearted, carelessly-generous, and genial of men, his great fault was weakness, and, with all his brilliance, a fatal want of judgment." She ends with a splendid series of Wilde's conversational epigrams (some of which he printed in *Intentions),* such as his famous opinion of Meredith:

> "Will you kindly tell me, Mr. Wilde, in your own words, your viewpoint of George Meredith?"
> "George Meredith is a prose Browning, and so is Browning."
> "Thank you. His style?"
> "Chaos, illuminated by flashes of lightning."

In this first third of the essay, Mrs. Leverson's method is one often used in novels, and especially in movies: she has given a panoramic view, then she has focused on this or that detail, and then she has centered upon where the view and the details have been carefully selected to lead her—upon the central human figure, Wilde himself.

The arrangement of the central section, "The Last First Night," follows another familiar literary form, which could be called the sandwich pattern, or the bracket effect. Mrs. Leverson begins with a description of one tonality and ends with one the same, or nearly the same; but between the two, the bulk of "The Last First Night" is a sharp contrast to the prologue and epilogue. The first sentences are: "On Valentine's Day, the 14th February 1895, there was a snow-storm more severe than had been remembered in London for years. A black, bitter, threatening wind blew the drifting snow. On that dark sinister winter's night . . ." and the last sentences are nearly identical.

Between this beginning and this end is a brilliant, light-filled evocation of the first night of *The Importance of Being Earnest* at the St. James's Theatre. Oscar had commanded that the flower of the evening be the lily-of-the-valley, and the stalls were filled with women whose large puffed sleeves were adorned with sprays of lilies and with young elegants whose boutonnieres were also that flower. "What a rippling, glittering, chattering crowd was that! . . . Whoever still lives who was present on that night will remember the continual ripple of laughter from the very first moment, the excitement, the strange almost hysterical joy with which was received this 'Trivial Comedy for Serious People.' . . ."

Wilde had arranged a box for the Sphinx and her friends, who included Mabel and Aubrey Beardsley, and she tells of his visit to the box between acts. She remembers his words, and she recalls with astonishing vividness his manner and physical appearance:

> He was on this evening at the zenith of his careless, genial career, beaming and filled with that *euphoria* that was curiously characteristic of him when he was not in actual grief or pain. He had a low wide brow, with straight heavy hair into which the iron had entered, thus giving him the look of a Roman bust. His face was a clear red-brown from a long stay by the sea. He had blue-grey eyes and a well-formed mouth curved by a perpetual smile, and often a laugh of sincere humorous enjoyment of life. He had a superb vitality, a short-sighted joy in living for the moment.
>
> . . .
>
> He was dressed with elaborate dandyism and a sort of florid sobriety. His coat had a black velvet collar. He held white gloves in his small pointed hands. On one finger he wore a large scarab ring. A green carnation, echo in colour of the ring, bloomed in his buttonhole, and a large bunch of seals on a black moiré ribbon watch-chain hung from his white waistcoat. This costume, which on another man might have appeared perilously like fancy dress, and on his imitators was nothing less, seemed to suit him perfectly; he seemed at ease and to have the look of the last gentleman in Europe.

"The last gentleman in Europe" is not only richly allusive; the phrase and its key word *last* lead her to the end of the essay, the mention of "the strange behaviour of the Marquess of Queensberry, who had left at the box-office an extraordinary bouquet of carrots, cauliflowers, turnips and other vegetables," and the return to the original description: "It was a freezing cold night, and a black bitter wind blew on Valentine's Day, the 14th February 1895, that date of the last first night."

The first two sections of the essay are static, but the third,

"Afterwards," has considerable narrative interest. It covers the Sphinx's relationship with Wilde from the time of his first trial in early 1895 until his death in 1900. The central section concerns, of course, the Leversons' granting asylum to Wilde during the period between his trials. Most biographies of Wilde during his latter years have made use of this part of Mrs. Leverson's memoir, and the events are too well known to warrant more than a summary: the loyalty of the Leversons' servants to them and to Wilde, his residence on the nursery floor, the arrangements made for his escape from England and his rejection of them, his two years' incarceration in prison, his reunion with the Sphinx and other friends on the morning of his release, his final years in Paris and the Sphinx's last visit with him there.

Into the narrative line she works many a small, vivid glimpse of Wilde, examples of his wit, his generosity, his capacity for sympathy and for sorrow. For biographical interest, this last part of the memoir is remarkable. Her artistry has a great moment at the end when she is witty, in no callous way, even if her subject is his death; and the wit is, generously, not her own, but Wilde's, and from his last play:

> One of the hits in *The Importance of Being Earnest* is when the clergyman says that Mr. Bunbury expressed a desire to be buried in Paris. "I fear," says the clergyman, "that this doesn't seem a very desirable state of mind at the last."
>
> Oscar is buried in Paris under Epstein's magnificent monument given, ten years after his death, by a lady[12] whose friendship remained steadfast to the end.

CHAPTER 5

# The Twelfth Hour

## I *Matter for a May Morning*

"IT was just about twelve o'clock, a lovely warm morning. The first hum of the season was just beginning, like the big orchestra of London tuning up. There seemed a sort of suppressed excitement in the air" (195). These sentences establish the mood of Mrs. Leverson's first novel, *The Twelfth Hour*, published in 1907. The entire novel seems to take place on "one gay irresponsible April afternoon" (138); it is clearly a first novel, not only in certain technical inexpertnesses, but, also, overcoming these, and in fact dependent on them, in its joyful, careless, sun-filled atmosphere.

In this story, atmosphere is everything: its closest comparison, one which the title itself suggests, is with Shakespeare's *Twelfth Night*, which is itself "matter for a May morning" and where we never for a moment doubt that all will go well. That Viola will win the Duke, we know from the first statement of her interest in him, just as we know that Felicity, heroine of *The Twelfth Hour*, will not lose her husband and that her sister Sylvia will get the husband she wants. We also know that, in fact, this happy world will never be for more than a moment darkened.

The delight is Mrs. Leverson's own—in London, in the freedom of her first large work of fiction, in the jokes she can make, in the amusing oddities of character she can recount, even in the very carelessness of meandering plot and functionless character. Although this novel is indeed a "gay irresponsible" one, just as there are undercurrents in *Twelfth Night*, so are there, in *The Twelfth Hour*, certain deeper concerns. They center around love and courtship and marriage. Especially the last: the "twelfth hour" is that last moment when Felicity's one-year-old marriage is saved. If it was never in any grave danger, it can serve as paradigm for what happens in marriages that are not, finally, saved and where endings are not so predictably happy as they are here. Mr. MacInnes has spoken of "the harrowing skill with which the tragedy, as yet undeclared, can be suddenly and dangerously seen (although in fact . . . it is to be prevented at 'the twelfth hour' by the husband and wife's moment of self-realisation. . . .");[1] but I feel this states the theme too heavily. *The Twelfth Hour* in its lightness is the one of Mrs. Leverson's novels most deserving the name of "soufflé"—a term used by a dozen reviewers of her books ("charlotte russe" has also been employed, and even "puff pastry").

If *The Twelfth Hour* is a fairy tale without villains, its heroines are impossibly pretty; its heroes, "excessively handsome." The nearest to an ogre we have is a Greek banker, Mr. Ridokanaki; but he turns out to be the fairy godmother by making possible Sylvia's marriage to Woodville—of whom Ridokanaki says with some bitterness, "He thinks I'm the Frog Prince and he's Prince Charming" (124). The very fact that Ridokanaki is not merely a millionaire, or even a billionaire, but, preposterously, a trillionaire, is one of those hyperboles which characterize every aspect of fairy tales. Mrs. Leverson's novels, and especially *The Twelfth Hour,* invariably have to a greater or less degree this quality of hyperbole—a simplifying, escapist, anti-Realist quality—no matter what complex insights into ordinary human experience they offer. One reviewer has said that "here is society as it would like to be seen and read about. . . ."[2] Her people are as stylized as they are stylish.

Another reviewer once pointed out that Mrs. Leverson's comedy could not survive World War I: such wit as hers "has not bloomed again after the blight of a World War. The 'brilliant, flippant, independent upper' class that George Meredith demanded as the protagonists of comedy have not survived."[3] Everyone seems to be very rich in *The Twelfth Hour* except for poor Woodville, and his poverty is disposed of with the absurdly high salary of £3,000 a year offered to him by the absurdly generous Mr. Ridokanaki. The upper-class, even aristocratic glitter of *The Twelfth Hour,* where titles are much more frequent than in any of the later novels, is a fairy-tale glitter; and emeralds, chinchilla wraps, gunmetal limousines studded with sapphires, and bouquets of mauve orchids are fitting images for, just as they are a part of, its rococo unrealism. It is exact concern with money that can make a novel realistic, as Edith and Bruce Ottley's financial problems in later novels prove. But in *The Twelfth Hour,* if Savile is down to his last shilling, Aunt William quickly gives him five pounds. It is perhaps Mrs. Leverson herself who is the fairy godmother.

## II *The Fairy Tale*

Many a critic has asserted that Mrs. Leverson's plots are episodic, inconsequential, or otherwise weak, and most of them have admitted that such weaknesses make no difference. Raymond Mortimer has said it best: "The plots would be almost substantial enough for short stories. But then the charm of these novels is their absurd insubstantiality."[4] Nonetheless, the power of the theme lends the plot of *The Twelfth Hour* an intermittent substantiality. The principal actions are a marriage rescued (Felicity and Chetwode's) and a marriage made (Sylvia and Woodville's). Minor characters contribute to the marriage theme by the parallels or parodies that their particular situations suggest.

Felicity has been married to Lord Chetwode for a year, and the glamour of early love survives. Unfortunately, Chetwode is never at home; he is either at auctions or at races—"spending at Christie's what he's lost at Kempton" (14)—and he regards his wife, the Watteau-like mistress of his Park Street mansion, as simply the finest of his bibelots. Despite her beauty and frivolity, Felicity has the real concern of making romance last into, or despite, marriage: a goal that is much more deeply explored by Bertha Kellynch in *Bird of Paradise.*

Felicity permits herself to flirt with gay young Bertie Wilton, who responds to the infatuated extent of, on his first visit, kissing her violently. Upon discovering a portrait of Blanche Tregelly, wife of a friend of Chetwode's, among Chetwode's possession, Felicity becomes jealous enough to question Chetwode, who detests scenes and who is not in the least interested in Mrs. Tregelly. In turn, Chetwode has let signs of restlessness creep into his usually imperturbable mien because of Bertie's assiduous courtship: and, when both sets of jealousy are brought into the open at the twelfth hour, the clouds lift and happiness is reestablished. The marriage-manual maxim apparently here dramatized is, "Communicate fully with your spouse." No secrets, no suspicions, should exist unspoken.

Sylvia, Felicity's younger sister, is in love with Woodville, her father's secretary; but they cannot be married because, though Sylvia will come into a fortune when she is twenty-one, Woodville himself is virtually penniless, having been disinherited by his uncle. Another of Sylvia's suitors, the fifty-year-old Greek trillionaire Ridokanaki, learns of Sylvia and Woodville's love; and, acting as *deus ex machina,* he gives Woodville a splendid job. The novel ends with Sylvia's marriage to Woodville.

A host of minor characters, a few too many, support the theme. Savile, the sixteen-year-old brother of Felicity and Sylvia, is minor only in a legal sense; he is probably the best-drawn character in the book. Although in love with the elderly Madame Patti (whom he has never met), he also courts the fourteen-year-old Dolly Clive; Savile's worship of the aged diva and his patronizing toleration of Dolly's interest in him are a humorous juvenile contrast to the more ordinary loves of his sisters Felicity and Sylvia.

Another contrast is supplied by Vera Ogilvie. A foolish woman, browbeaten by her husband, and given to fantastic costumes of Japanese draperies and long earrings, Mrs. Ogilvie longs for love, and she fixes on Captain Henderson, a horsy clubman type, as a candidate. Captain Henderson, however, plays the field; in the past, he has flirted with an intense red-haired intellectual girl named Lucy Winter, who in turn fastens her affections upon the demure author F. J. Rivers. Currently, Captain Henderson is most interested in "Agatha, Mrs. Wilkinson"—so called because she has no title—who is as devoted to the turf as he is. Jasmyn Vere, a rich middle-aged esthete, cherishes a passion for Agatha. Vera Ogilvie's yearning for love is temporarily assuaged by the sudden devotion of Mr. Newman Ferguson, who unfortunately turns out to be a raving lunatic, to Felicity's and even Vera's amusement. The concentric circles of true, false, and putative lovers surround Felicity, who has been married twelve months, and Sylvia, who is about to be married. Undoubtedly some of these characters are not integral, and their presence insists on the theme repetitively. But each is more or less comic in his own way; one guesses at the real-life prototypes whom Mrs. Leverson found funny.

What unites the large cast, and what in fact organizes the novel, is jealousy. The word itself runs like a leitmotiv through the novel. Vera Ogilvie is jealous of Captain Henderson's interest in Mrs. Wilkinson, just as Jasmyn Vere is jealous of Mrs. Wilkinson's interest in Captain Henderson. Bertie is jealous of Felicity's admiration for the composer De Valdez (who is to reappear years later in the last of Mrs. Leverson's novels, *Love at Second Sight*), while Woodville, "subject to acute, almost morbid, attacks of physical jealousy" (54), resents any man who looks at Sylvia. Savile is jealous of Dolly Clive's young French friend, Robert de Saules, while Dolly is jealous of Savile's attachment to "the Other Girl"—Madame Patti: "Then I'll try not to be jealous of her. I won't think about her at all" (251). But their jealousies are what they do think about.

The majority of novels that deal with marriage—it is tempting to say sweepingly the majority of novels—cover the year or so before marriage. *The Twelfth Hour* concerns the year after, when the romance of courtship lingers, but when the question of whether or not the marriage will become a true one has demandingly arisen. Felicity and Chetwode still view each other with the illusory glamour of courtship—they are "far more like lovers than husband and wife" (231)—but jealousy, on both sides, acts as a catalyst to precipitate a more solid relationship.

The central process of *The Twelfth Hour* is the twin awakening of jealousy in Felicity and her husband Chetwode. When Chetwode suggests that Bertie Wilton bring Felicity home from a party he himself is not attending, she thinks, "Was there a tone of irony in his voice? Could he be a shade jealous? How delightful!" (206). And later, "Driving along, Felicity thought, 'Perhaps if Chetwode *could* be made a shade jealous of Bertie, it might be a good thing. Still that sort of thing is so commonplace. We oughtn't to have to descend to it" (214). She rebels against the leveling influence of this universal emotion: " 'Are any of those eternal vulgar theories about love ever really true?' Then wasn't Chetwode superior? Of course he was. That was why she loved him, and in wishing him to be an ordinary jealous man, she was wishing him to descend" (214–15). Yet later, Felicity asks Madam Zero, the Irish-American soothsayer, " 'I should like to know . . . whether the person I care for is true to me.' As she said the words she thought they sounded as if she were a sentimental shop-girl whose young man had shown signs of ceasing his attentions. And why not? She felt exactly like that shop-girl. It was precisely the same thing" (238).

The "descent"—as she thinks of it—of the Watteau marquise into a "shop-girl" is a metaphor for Felicity's descent from romance to realism. Her love was first a fairy-tale love; but, after the refinements of jealousy have instructed her, hers is a much more practical and meaningful human love. In the successful marriage, cloud-cuckoo romance is converted into a soberer, deeper relation—or so Mrs. Leverson seems to say. This lesson is no longer fairy tale; it is what the novel—if only semi-consciously and sporadically—intelligently teaches. Mrs. Leverson was only half aware of her own theme, we feel, but this fact does not invalidate its interest.

## III *Characters and Caricatures*

Felicity's quest, to learn how love can be preserved after marriage, would be more compelling if she were less idealized as a character. Statements like "From the age of two Felicity had been an acknowledged beauty" (8) and "Felicity's view of life was that it was great fun" (63) have, beyond the mere data they convey, a rhetorically distancing effect. She is too pretty and too elegant; and she is both too shallow and too wise: shallow enough to flirt with the foppish Bertie Wilton, she is wise enough to be the confidante and arbiter of her friends' love problems.

Throughout her novels Mrs. Leverson moves in and out of her characters' minds at will; for, despite her admiration for the novels of Henry James, she seems to have learned little of the value of carefully controlling the point of view. But with Lord Chetwode, as if by novelistic instinct, she stumbles on an effective device to make him more interesting than Felicity and to supply some suspense to the plot: he is dramatized, our view of him is almost always external, and we can only guess what he basically thinks of Felicity's flirtation with Bertie. Even if his interest in horses—there are many knowledgeable turf details in the novel—is clearly taken from Ernest Leverson's own passion for the track, Chetwode is seen with wit and detachment: "He was a good-looking, amiable, and wealthy young man, who was as lavish as if he had not had a penny . . ." (9). His chief mania is for collecting art, and the way in which a collector can come to regard people as objects which are owned—Felicity is his finest—is presented as his inevitable *idée fixe*. He is not a great character, but he is a successful one.

Mrs. Leverson's heroes and heroines are not, with an exception here and there, her great characters: they are too symbolic or allegorized or idealized. The other pair of young lovers, Sylvia and Woodville, also lack major interest. Although we see in Sylvia the wholehearted devotion of a young girl for her intended—a devotion almost cruel in its purity, although she has individualizing traits of obstinacy (inherited from her father) and frivolity (an echo of her sister's)—there is too much talk about her and not enough of her in action to illustrate what she basically is. For example, we have the fine observation of how she runs her father's household: "she would receive excuses from servants with a smile so sweet yet so incredulous that it disarmed deceit and made incompetence hide its head (or give notice)" (34). Mrs. Leverson is better on Sylvia's physical appearance than on her mental characteristics—and once again, the reason is that Mrs. Leverson tends to stylize her heroines out of existence: "The iron had obviously entered into her hair (or into every seventh wave, at least, of her hair), and her dresses fitted her as a flower its sheath. She was natural, but not in the least wild; no primrose by a river's brim, nor an artificial bloom, but rather a hothouse flower just plucked and very carefully wired."

Of Sylvia's lover, Woodville, we do not know much more than that he loves Sylvia. Having had great expectations of inheriting £20,000 a year from his uncle, Woodville has been rendered almost penniless. His uncle, "instead of making his wife his housekeeper, as most men do . . . made his housekeeper his wife. She was a depressing woman. In a year he had a son and heir, and within two months after this event, he died, leaving his nephew exactly one hundred pounds a year" (29). Woodville's frustrations, both economic and sexual, are shown in detail, as are his gentlemanliness and his sense of the proprieties; but his attributes seem hung on a tailor's dummy. His nature is too unmixed to be credible.

Mrs. Leverson is better at minor characters because she is a creator of comic types, and there is something Dickensian in the vitality of Savile, his father Sir James, and his Aunt William (as children Felicity and Sylvia and Savile gave her this name; her husband, now dead, they called Uncle Mary). Some critics would add Bertie Wilton, but, though we can see him vividly as "an agreeable rattle," he is too effeminate to be convincing as Felicity's ardent wooer. He is an authority on lady's hats, and he even designs a dress for her (gold, to rhyme with her golden hair), but the contrast of his febrile fancifulness with Chetwode's quiet masculinity, while it makes it credible that Felicity's own frivolity would be momentarily attracted to Bertie's, renders unbelievable the passionate love he declares. Another contrast between the two men lies in Chetwode's collection of permanent works of art and Bertie's interest in the ephemeral, such as fashion and gossip.

A great comic character of Dickens, like Micawber, is highly repetitious and self-absorbed; he is a paradigm of a human trait or two raised to magnificent intensity. In contrast, we have Mrs. Leverson's Sir James Crofton:

"No hurry, no hurry," said Sir James, with that air of self-denial that conveys the urgent necessity of intense speed. He was a handsome old man, with thick grey hair, a white military moustache, bushy dark eyebrows, and in his eyes that humorous twinkle that is so often seen in those men of the last generation who are most devoid of a sense of humour. Sir James was liable to the irritable changes of mood that would nowadays be called neurotic or highly strung, but was in his young days merely put down as bad temper. He had a high estimation of his mental powers, and a poor opinion of those who did not share this estimation. . . . His contemporaries liked him: at least, they smiled when his name was mentioned. He was warm-hearted and generous; he had a curious mania for celebrities; was a hospitable host, a tedious guest, and a loyal friend. His late wife (who was lovely, but weary) had always described him in one word. The word was "trying." (24–25)

The difference between the portrayals of Mrs. Leverson and Dickens is that Sir James has more traits; therefore, though he is a type, he is much less specific a type. He lies between the complexity of a fully human character and the simplicity of a Dickens figure, with the result that he is not so ordinarily believable as the first nor so intensely compelling as the second.

Aunt William, who is "a small, pointed person, with a depressing effect of having (perhaps) been a beauty once" (41), and who complains to her maid in the morning that "she had had insomnia for twenty minutes" (43), is best seen in the house she lives in, the description of which has been quoted earlier in Chapter 2, and in her relationships with other matrons among her acquaintance and with her nephew Savile. There are several battles among rich elderly women in Mrs. Leverson's novels—they could be called the "Dowager Wars"—and there is a good one, too lengthy to quote, in *The Twelfth Hour* between Aunt William and "a very old and dear friend of hers whom she particularly disliked and disapproved of, Lady Virginia Harper" (292–93). With her nephew Savile, who "was really more at home with Aunt William than with any one, even his sisters" (44), she is uncritical, indulgent, and fascinated:

> "I shall have to be going now, Aunt William. Got an appointment."
> "With whom, my dear?"
> "Yes," said Savile dryly. . . .
> "Ah, I see!" she said knowingly (wishing she did). (48)
>
> . . .
>
> Before he left, Aunt William pressed a sovereign into his hand guiltily, as if it were conscience money. He, on his side, took it as though it were a doctor's fee, and both ignored the transaction. (49)
>
> . . .
>
> "Yes. Get along with you, and I do hope that you won't turn out a dreadful, extravagant fast young man when you're grown up," said Aunt William, with relish at the idea. (265)

Some adult suggests to Savile that he will probably one day be prime minister. This extraordinary sixteen-year-old Etonian has such aplomb that he can make most adults feel hopelessly ineffectual. He is a manager: he brings Chetwode home to Felicity when she misses him; he tries to find a position for Woodville; he protects Sylvia from compromising herself by a visit to Woodville's studio. Generally gifted with "an air of more self-control than seemed required for the occasion" (8), Savile's one weakness is his adoration of Madame Patti. The last lines of the book, which concern Sylvia's wedding to Woodville, are deservedly given to him: "Savile's attitude as best man was of such extraordinary correctness that it was the feature of the ceremony, and even distracted public attention from the bridegroom" (309).

*The Twelfth Hour* is the most skillful of Mrs. Leverson's novels in providing a sense of family. Not only Aunt William's indulgence of Savile but also Savile's patronizing of his sisters, Sir James's pride in Sylvia's obstinacy, so like his own, and Felicity's older-sister authority with Sylvia establish recognizable family patterns. They can sometimes be pinpointed as autobiographical; for example, Aunt William is based on the second wife—"the grey-haired daughter of a dignitary of the Church of England"—of George Leverson, Ernest's father;[5] and her devotion to Savile mirrors Mrs. Leverson's own fondness for and understanding of schoolboys.[6] One final comparison needs to be made with Dickens: Dickens' characters, even when they are man and wife, can give the odd impression of being perfectly unacquainted; but the ways in which Mrs. Leverson's characters know one another—listen to, react to, comment upon one another—help us to become closely acquainted with them and thereby to be convinced by and interested in their behavior.

## IV *As a First Novel*

Such typical aspects of Mrs. Leverson's novels as the wit, the preponderance of dialogue, the union of comedy of manners and domestic romance, and the theme of marriage, as well as other subjects, are already present in *The Twelfth Hour.* But other characteristics mark it clearly as her first long work. Never a Flaubert, Mrs. Leverson in *The Twelfth Hour* treats the scene of Felicity's and Chetwode's mutual expression of jealousy as *scène obligatoire;* but the parallel resolution between Sylvia and Woodville, the path to their marriage cleared by Ridokanaki's generosity, is barely developed. Despite the general atmosphere of confetti and happily-ever-after at the conclusion, loose ends abound: Vera Ogilvie may laugh at the admiration she has excited in a madman, but there is no indication she has learned; and will Jasmyn Vere continue his unlucky pursuit of Agatha, Mrs. Wilkinson?—and will Lucy Winter acquire F. J. Rivers for her very own? Nor is there the sense of life's familiar irresolution in these loose ends; Mrs. Leverson merely forgot them, or they had ceased to interest her.

In her later novels, there are also plot-pointless figures like the actor Arthur Mervyn in the present novel, but they are often justifiable in their own comic right, as Arthur Mervyn is not. More believably dangerous threats to a marriage than Bertie Wilton make their appearance, like Harry de Freyne in *The Limit* or Nigel Hillier in *Bird of Paradise,* not to mention the various women who find Bruce Ottley easy prey in the three Ottley novels. Human manipulation resolves plots, not Greek trillionaires.

The comedy, as I hope the passages I have quoted confirm, has already its own delightful note, that sound of subdued absurd hilarity unique with Mrs. Leverson. There are epigrams, such as "everything comes to the man who won't wait" (160); and there are sharp paradoxical character summaries: "As a matter of fact, nothing Agatha did was ever noticed, because she never did anything that was not extraordinary" (213). But the element of pure joke is less successful in *The Twelfth Hour,* for example, the opposition to education among the Crofton children: "Savile would never eat *Reading* biscuits, because he feared that some form of condensed study was being insidiously introduced into the system" (41; italics not mine). There is some fairly crude dialect humor, such as the butler Greenstock who complains of his " 'harsthma' (so he pronounced it)" (7), and a tedious Cockney guide in the chapter "Madame Tussaud's."

Even with Mrs. Leverson's skill in dialogue, there are one or two false steps in *The Twelfth Hour,* empty exchanges, flat repartee. There is a cross-purpose conversation (130 ff.) in which Felicity is speaking of Bertie, Savile of Madame Patti—a purely theatrical technique, here inexpertly applied, to be much refined in her later work. Mrs. Leverson's direct addresses to the reader are often singularly sly and charming, but the humor of a passage like the following, with its pointed alliteration, is heavy:

> Was there then, some other attraction, something that outweighed, transcended for him all the petty pangs and penalties of his position?
>
> This arch surmise of the writer will be found by the persevering reader to be perfectly reasonable and founded on fact.

Such criticism may be captious. One or two of the first reviews expressed bewilderment: the *Bookman,* for example, said, "We . . . have only hazy ideas as to what it is all about. . . ,"[7] but the prevailing reaction was a highly enthusiastic one. The *Westminster Gazette* praised Savile as "the gem of a work which contains many delightful sketches of character,"[8] and the *Academy* said, among much else that was favorable, that Mrs. Leverson's characters "are not taken from other books but from people."[9]

To a modern reader, *The Twelfth Hour* seems an unusual accomplishment for a first novel becauses it consistently strikes its own note, has its own unique and realized world, and betrays no divided aim or uncertainty or hesitation. Though far from perfect, no book is perfect; and this novel still has today a May-morning freshness.

CHAPTER 6

# Love's Shadow

## I *As A Second Novel*

ALTHOUGH published only a year after Mrs. Leverson's first novel, *Love's Shadow*, which appeared in 1908, is clearly an advance. It lacks the euphoric joy which bathes the people and places of *The Twelfth Hour* in an atmosphere of gilded never-never land, but what it loses in ornamentation it makes up for in design. The epigraph from Shakespeare suggests the design:

> Love like a shadow flies
> When substance love pursues;
> Pursuing that that flies
> And flying what pursues.

Cecil Reeve, who is at least nominally the hero, has been in love with the widow Eugenia Raymond for years. She is not his mistress: she is forty-four and he is thirty-four; she treats him—sometimes tolerantly, sometimes impatiently—like the silly, importunate boy he acts. At one point, when his attentions have become particularly insistent, she tells him with the friendly frankness that is one of her most attractive features that she has been hopelessly in love with Sir Charles Cannon for years; and she urges him to let himself fall in love with Sir Charles's ward, the heiress Hyacinth Verney, the nominal heroine of the novel. He does; but the shadow of his old passion for Eugenia hangs over his marriage to Hyacinth, even after Eugenia herself is married—and to Cecil's uncle Lord Selsey, whom Cecil idolizes and models himself after, and whose heir he is. Earlier, Cecil has discussed his infatuation for Eugenia with his uncle, and he is embittered by his uncle's quick victory where he had been defeated for years.

But it is not so much on the rebound that Cecil marries Hyacinth as because he has begun to fall in love with her—chiefly, it might seem, because she is so much in love with him: what might be called the echo-effect in love. Some months after she has become Cecil's bride, Hyacinth, aware that there is a "shadow" over her marriage (206), thinks she discovers that Cecil is continuing a liaison with "that creature"—now his aunt—Lady Selsey. But he convinces her, more by an appeal to her love than to her logic, that her suspicions are unfounded (which they are not); and the novel ends ironically with Cecil's magnanimously forgiving her. Love's shadow is not only Cecil's long attachment to Eugenia, for late in the novel the title assumes additional meaning: "Yes, his fancy for Eugenia was the shadow, a will-o'-the-wisp; Hyacinth was the reality—a very lovely and loving reality" (274).

Since it is, of course, possible for a man to love more than one woman at the same time, Cecil's story has an interesting psychological foundation. In the uncle, whose heir he is, he has a father figure whose sophistication he can admire and imitate; in Eugenia, he has had a mother figure—she says, with her own kind of sophisticated exaggeration, "You know perfectly well—I'm sure I make no secret of it—that I'm ten years older than you. Old enough to be your mother!" (44). Her marriage to his uncle is thus the classic Freudian betrayal, and Cecil passes through his identity crisis by marrying—not his mother—but a woman suitably younger than he. Presumably this *rite de passage* constitutes his entry into maturity.

The plot of *Love's Shadow* is, therefore, not divided between two couples—as it is in *The Twelfth Hour*, where it shuttles back and forth with amiable inconsequence—but centers on a single couple, Cecil and Hyacinth. However, nearly half of the book is devoted to Bruce and Edith Ottley, who have been married for three years. The chapters that concern the young Ottleys are the most vivid account imaginable of a marriage between unequals. Bruce is a monster of egotism, but Edith, twice as intelligent, is endlessly patient, though observed with too much wit, and herself too witty, to be saccharine. Romance has gone and the breakfast table talk concerns bills, illness, the cook, the office, and so forth.

Why are the Ottleys in the novel? They are little connected

with the main events in the plot, though Edith is Hyacinth's close friend and confidante and though Bruce precipitates an event or two when he tells Lady Cannon that her husband's ward Hyacinth has been seen holding hands in the park with Cecil. Lady Cannon is officiously horrified and takes it upon herself to warn Hyacinth that her behavior is not respectable. Hyacinth reacts with anger, and Cecil almost becomes engaged to Hyacinth because Lady Cannon asks if he is. But the Ottleys' part in the novel is essentially static and, in terms of the narrative proper, extraneous.

What they do supply more concretely is a contrast in tonality. The humdrum trivia of married life are posed against the romance of Hyacinth and Cecil. Not everyone is very rich or about to be in *Love's Shadow,* as was the case in *The Twelfth Hour.* Bruce says,

> "Edith, I want you to look nice to-night, dear; what are you going to wear?"
> "My Other Dress," said Edith. (48)

But Hyacinth is an heiress, one who, as her companion Anne Yeo thinks, looks "too romantic for everyday life" (15). In *Love's Shadow,* the dichotomy of realism and romance observed in *The Twelfth Hour* is intensified by the contrast between the prosaic disillusionment of Edith's marriage and the poetic intensity of Hyacinth's.

From another standpoint, the theme of the novel is suitability in marriage. Cecil and Hyacinth belong together in their looks, money, and personalities; Mrs. Raymond's marriage to Lord Selsey unites two sophisticated older people, and her wit complements his erudition. Sir Charles and Lady Cannon are mismatched, and Bruce and Edith are disastrously unsuited: shallowness contrasts to depth; querulousness, to mildness; self-delusion, to objectivity. The quality which Sir Charles and Edith both exemplify and which keeps their marriages from foundering is patience.

This firmer grasp of theme is repeated in other components of the novel. There are fewer extraneous characters; and the dialogue is less airy but more sophisticated. Two of the most intelligent people in the novel are Sir Charles Cannon and Anne Yeo. Speaking of Lady Cannon, Sir Charles says:

"And if she does a thing that's disagreeable to her, she likes to do it in the most painful possible way. She has a beautiful nature."

Anne smiled, and passed him a little gold box.

"Have a cigarette?" she suggested.

"Thanks—I'm not really in a bad temper." (19–20)

And of Edith, Sir Charles comments:

"I suppose she amuses Hyacinth?"

"Yes; of course, she's not a dull old maid over forty, like me," said Anne.

"No one would believe that description of you," said Sir Charles, with a bow that was courtly but absent. As a matter of fact, he did believe it, but it wasn't true. (20)

As the last sentence just quoted shows, Mrs. Leverson's authorial comments are leaner and quicker. A reviewer in the *Times Literary Supplement* said of Mrs. Leverson that, "although associated with the Nineties as contributor to the *Yellow Book*, her style has an economy and directness that belong to a later and more coherent school."[1] But at her best she sounds neither Edwardian nor modern but simply like herself. Of Hyacinth, she says, "So many artistic young men had told her she was like La Gioconda, that when she first saw the original in the Louvre she was so disappointed that she thought she would never smile again" (18). And, for a final example, we have Anne, who is now speaking with Hyacinth:

"No one can speak of me as 'that pleasant, cultivated creature who lives with Miss Verney,' can they?"

"Not, at any rate, if they have any regard for truth," said Hyacinth. (27)

The wit of *Love's Shadow* is less ebullient than that of *The Twelfth Hour*, but it is never silly or private; it is more closely based on character; it is less Wildean, less journalistic, and more "characteristic."

## II *The Central Hyacinth*

Neither Hyacinth nor Cecil is free of the glamour of idealization which makes Felicity, Chetwode, Sylvia, and Woodville in *The Twelfth Hour* like figures in an eighteenth-century dance.

Although we are told of Cecil's intelligence and although his maturation is completely interesting, he pales into insignificance as a character when contrasted with, for example, Bruce Ottley. Anne Yeo's opinion of Cecil is a clue to what is missing in him as a character: "It vexed her particularly that Hyacinth fancied Cecil so unusual, while she was very certain that there were thousands and thousands of good-looking young men in England who had the same education, who were precisely like him. There was not a pin to choose between them" (177).

Hyacinth's problems are real, but she is too beautiful, too rich, too primary. "All the men are more or less in love with Hyacinth. . . . Even the women are attracted by her," wrote an early reviewer of the novel.[2] We know Hyacinth better than we know Sylvia Crofton in *The Twelfth Hour,* but still too abstractly. The weakest passage in the novel is the conversation between Cecil and Hyacinth at her dinner party (54 ff.), a dull flirtation. Yet she is the center of the novel, and into her orbit the other characters are drawn by love or by jealousy—which is an even more potent force in the emotional life of the characters here than it was in *The Twelfth Hour.*

The three grand grotesques of the novel, each a part of the love-jealousy matrix, are Anne Yeo, Lady Cannon, and Bruce Ottley. Like Falstaff or Shylock, these three are so compellingly realized that they steal the spotlight from the nominal hero and heroine and threaten to break the bounds of the work that contains them.

Anne Yeo, whom Stevie Smith has called "an astonishing portrait for the period,"[3] could have come out of a novel written yesterday; she is a superb psychosexual study which has none of the grimness we often associate with that genre. Mrs. Leverson's description of Anne is brilliantly economical: "With a rather wooden face, high cheek-bones, a tall, thin figure, and no expression, Anne might have been any age; but she was not. She made every effort to look quite forty so as to appear more suitable as a chaperone, but was in reality barely thirty" (15).

Anne is usually seen in outlandish garb: "she wore a golf cap, thick boots, and a mackintosh, although it was a beautiful day" (94). Of her background, we know that her family was not interested in her, that she has an inherited income of £500 a year, and that "from her earliest youth she had hated and despised all men that she had known" (176). To many, she is only Hyacinth's parsimonious, eccentric, and comic companion, but beneath her pose of shrewd cynic lies the secret of her love for Hyacinth. Like Viola in *Twelfth Night,* Anne cannot stifle the expression of her love, but Hyacinth, like Viola's love Orsino, is too absorbed in herself and in romantic love to take cognizance:

> "Why do you think Bruce tried to make mischief in this horrid way?"
> "Only because he's a fool. Like so many of us, he's in love with you," said Anne.
> Hyacinth laughed, thinking Anne was in fun. (117)

Inevitably, Anne despises Cecil, and she mysteriously disappears at the time of the wedding, but returns, by love's instinct, when the marriage is beginning to go badly. When Hyacinth sees Cecil with Eugenia, the magnanimity of Anne's conduct shows how the highest love can forget jealousy; by a visit to Eugenia, she succeeds in healing the rift. Eugenia and Lord Selsey leave for a long cruise in the Greek islands, during which Hyacinth and Cecil's marriage will surely, after its shaky beginnings, learn to flourish. The last glimpse we have of Anne is in a sad and funny little paragraph: "She was on her way to Cook's. She had suddenly decided to emigrate" (300).

Anne's frustration in love is a moving subplot in the novel; we do not like Hyacinth better for her ignorance of it; it is Cecil, surprisingly, that comes closest to awareness, when he accuses Hyacinth, "Upon my word, I believe you prefer her to me!" (265), although Eugenia also seems to have an intuition of the depth of Anne's devotion (271). Like Anne, the pleasant people in the novel can laugh at themselves, and they have some self-knowledge and some knowledge of others—like Eugenia and Edith and Sir Charles; Bruce alone is a sufficient example of the unpleasant type, of those who are as dense about themselves as they are about others. Anne knows that Bruce and Sir Charles are in love with Hyacinth; she resents Hyacinth's dependence on Edith; she can bring herself to treat Cecil generously. In fact, she has such believable and such high human qualities that her exit is not purely poignant; she has her toughness, her mad wit, and her golf cap, thick boots, and mackintosh.

The reader might think that the magnificent Lady Cannon

would be immune from the green-eyed monster, but Mrs. Leverson is more astute: "For Hyacinth she [Lady Cannon] always felt a curious mixture of chronic anger, family pride, and admiring disapproval, which combination she had never yet discovered to be a common form of vague jealousy" (109). Descriptions of her and of her drawing room have been quoted earlier in Chapter 2, but other glimpses round out the study:

She always held her head as if she were being photographed in a tiara *en profil perdu*. It was in this attitude that she had often been photographed and was now most usually seen; and it seemed so characteristic that even her husband, if he accidentally caught a glimpse of her full-face, hastily altered his position to one whence he could behold her at right angles.

As she grew older, the profile in the photographs had become more and more *perdu*; the last one showed chiefly the back of her head, besides a basket of flowers, and a double staircase, leading (one hoped) at least to one of the upper rooms in Buckingham Palace. (35)

Mrs. Leverson is equally deft in creating Lady Cannon's dialogue. A grand, cold, hard snob of a woman, with a reputation for sound common sense while she is in fact silly to the point of stupidity, she is especially preposterous in her sense of propriety, as when she says to her husband, " 'I've had a little' (she lowered her voice) 'lumbago . . .' " (38). She is too obtuse to have an inkling that her husband's interest in his ward Hyacinth is other than paternal and that Hyacinth's marriage to Cecil, no matter how well Sir Charles behaves at the ceremony (he is like Anne in his self-subjugation), is most painful to him:

"Ah, Charles, you have no romance. Doesn't the night of those happy young people bring back the old days?"

The door shut. Lady Cannon was alone.

"He has no soul," she said to herself, using a tiny powder-puff. (170)

If Lady Cannon is pure egoist, a stronger term must be used for Bruce Ottley. As well as being an egomaniac, he is suspicious, hypochondriac, envious, jealous, conceited, fatuous, self-important, childishly transparent: the list could go on and on, with such mastery does Mrs. Leverson present him. Yet we do not dislike him. We deplore him, certainly; and yet even when we deplore him, we are in effect deploring not Bruce but human nature. He is essentially a nonliterary creation so instantly are we familiar with him, and his vices are the daily ones, not the major sins of an Iago or a Richard III. The worst thing that we can say about him is that he is basically harmless. Since Mrs. Leverson gives him many pages, her interest seems nearly obsessive. If anywhere, her moral stance can be predicated on all the things that Bruce is not.

Bruce does not change in the subsequent Ottley novels, *Tenterhooks* and *Love at Second Sight,* although his wife Edith gradually assumes in those books the status of an ideal woman. Ordinarily terrible as Bruce is, Edith—and Mrs. Leverson—are tolerant of him. Mrs. Leverson's chief triumph in the creation of Bruce may be that this most boring of men never bores us. Nothing so appallingly lifelike can be boring. V. S. Pritchett has said of Bruce: "The most boring and self-centered of men, Bruce Ottley, thrives on boredom and develops, in consequence, a character so eccentric that it never ceases to fascinate his friends."[4]

From Edith, who finds Hyacinth the romance of her life, to Bruce, who is absurdly jealous of Cecil Reeve, Hyacinth controls the novel. She is not fascinating like Eugenia; she is not intelligent like Anne; she is not self-abnegating and patient and responsible like Edith: her business is to be a heroine. However, if we deprecate her relative lack of interest in comparison with these women, she nonetheless has more substantiality than either Felicity or Sylvia in *The Twelfth Hour.* And the novel adheres to her story as closely as Mr. Leverson was ever to adhere to a plot line. There are excrescences in *Love's Shadow,* like the amiable eccentric Raggett, who suddenly falls in love with Edith and as suddenly totally disappears from the novel; and there are transparently theatrical devices, like Hyacinth's overhearing a revealing conversation between Cecil and Eugenia, a sense of "Curtain" with the punch line at the end of chapters, and a quantity of dialogue for its own sake. But *Love's Shadow* is less lightweight than *The Twelfth Hour;* and, in plot, theme, character, and comedy, the second work is as good as any other novel that Mrs. Leverson wrote.

## CHAPTER 7

# The Limit

### I *Contemporary Reviews*

AN unusually large number of reviews of Mrs. Leverson's third novel, *The Limit*, have survived from 1911, the year of publication. The favorable reception that her novels received, whether in first or subsequent editions, has already been noted; and the following comments from contemporary critics can be taken as typical. For a writer who does not yet appear in some of the standard "comprehensive" literary histories, we are somewhat surprised to read that the reviewer of *The Limit* in the *Daily Telegraph* said simply that Mrs. Leverson "is possessed of a very rare and very perfect talent . . .",[1] while the writer in the *Star*, another newspaper, said that *The Limit* was "one of the wittiest novels I have ever read . . . her style is a miracle of dainty malice and delicate satire. . . . Mrs. Leverson is a consummate artist."[2] *Vanity Fair* found it "a very clever book, full of witty epigram";[3] the *Referee* said that "the book is bright and full of good things";[4] the *Graphic* commented on the novel's freshness, liveliness, and cleverness;[5] and the *Pelican* predicted that "If she is not careful she will find herself writing a very great story indeed. As it is, she has come near doing so in *The Limit*."[6] Both the *Morning Post*[7] and the *World*[8] praised especially the characterization.

It did not matter to the reviewer in the *World* that the story was thin, a point also made by the *Westminster Gazette*, which added that *The Limit* "has a faint flavour of the clever stories which were written for the 'Yellow Book' and its contemporaries, but it is neither tragic nor affected nor grotesque, as so much of that literature aimed at being."[9] The *Morning Leader* was still another periodical which pointed out that the novel had little plot and that "The perpetual levity becomes at times strained . . .";
but this reviewer also asserted that *The Limit* was nonetheless

"a very pleasant book. It is silly, but it is refreshingly silly."[10] The article in the *Standard* is the best written of all these early comments, and its remarks on the plot are a fine description of Mrs. Leverson's method in general:

> In "The Limit" there are half a dozen portraits at least that are brilliant in their incisive individuality. They have not, many of them, anything whatever to do with the story, but then that is Mrs. Leverson's way. She goes out for a walk and drags her characters after her, and plays indeed the impromptu showman to her friends, opening doors and windows, telling little stories about this person and that one, sketching little scenes and situations, and finally, with a smile and a bow, leaving you because it is tea-time.[11]

In 1911 the schism between the popular periodical and the intellectual periodical was much less marked than it is now. The eleven reviews from newspapers and popular magazines just quoted can be considered representative of the range of reaction. *The Limit*, like Mrs. Leverson's other five novels, received, therefore, a warm welcome.

## II *Antiheroics*

Among critics who have written on *The Limit* in recent years, Leo Lerman has recognized—and he seems close in spirit to the reviewer in the *Standard* quoted above—that plot is not what we read her novels for: "The Sphinx's plot, in *The Limit*, is as unimportant as it is in any of the other novels. She uses plot much in the manner of the best French *farceur*: a peg upon which to hang an especial view of society and its manners."[12]

When *Love's Shadow* and *The Limit* were reprinted by Chapman and Hall at the same time in 1950, comparisons between Mrs. Leverson's second and third novels were inevitably made, usually at the expense of the former. At the time of these reprints, Inez Holden had just written in the *Cornhill* that "*The Limit* is probably Mrs. Leverson's best novel. The story is lightly, wittily and, apparently, almost carelessly told, and yet within the framework of the Fancy Dress Ball there is a sort of secondary sadness."[13] The critic of the *Times Literary Supplement* wrote that "*The Limit* shows an advance in constructive powers on *Love's Shadow*,"[14] and Adrian Alington in *Public Opinion* said that "Of the two novels, *The Limit* is by far the better, principally because the deeper side of Ada Leverson's talent finds more scope."[15]

However, the most recent critic of Mrs. Leverson's books, Colin MacInnes, comes closer to the novel than earlier critics because he is more exact, and exacting, than they. Of the relative deficiencies of *The Limit,* he observes that "This book is more imperfect than some others: the 'plot' creaks at times, with 'coincidences' rather nonchalantly contrived; there is even, most unusually for Ada Leverson, some padding. . . ."[16] If *The Limit* is Mrs. Leverson's weakest novel, the basic reason is some weakness or frailty in intention. It may, indeed, allow scope for Mrs. Leverson's "deeper side", but in the helterskelter mélange of other intentions, or in the absence of any single intention, *The Limit* lacks the cohesion that mood or theme affords *The Twelfth Hour* and *Love's Shadow.*

Valentia Wyburn, the heroine of *The Limit,* is the crux of these considerations. It would be easier to point out her unattractive features and call her the antiheroine, just as it would be easy to call her husband Romer a dolt and her lover Harry a snake. But, in fact, as with Mrs. Leverson's other heroines, Valentia is idealized to the extent—she is obviously presented as an arbiter of common sense and elegance—that, in some respects, she is a highly attractive creature. She is so much cleverer than the other characters that our natural allegiance goes to her, and many critics have delighted in this "sunbeam" of a woman, full of observant cynicism, stylish and flippant, and composed. One or two have said that she is a vain and frivolous young woman and have made an easy transition into vanity and frivolity as the hallmarks of Mrs. Leverson's silver-gilt world.

Yet the case against Valentia—whether or not Mrs. Leverson, let alone her critics, realized it—is damning. The question broached in the earlier novels, of whether or not romance is still possible after marriage, is answered by Valentia with: yes—with another man. Her friend Vaughan warns her, "It's really too distressingly conventional of you to suppose that because you happen to be legally married there can be no sort of romance" (266), and he means with her husband. But it takes more than good advice to bring Valentia to her senses.

She has been married to her husband Romer for five years—the longest of any young couple so far encountered in the novels.

When we meet her, she is carrying on a liaison with her cousin, Harry de Freyne,[17] an artist *manqué* but an expert lover. Valentia explains to a stranger, with suggestive ambiguity, that Harry "is an artist too . . . but—well, not in any of the recognized arts" (249). The relationship of Valentia with her husband Romer is summarized by the first words in the novel:

> "Romer, are you listening?"
> "Valentia, do I ever do anything else?" (11)

The truth is that Romer has made an idol of his wife. The point of view with regard to Romer is controlled in the same way as it is with Lord Chetwode in *The Twelfth Hour:* at the beginning of the novel, we are inside his mind long enough to see his worship of his wife; throughout most of the novel, we see him only externally, silent or monosyllabic; at the end of the novel, we again enter his mental processes to see the agony of his jealousy of Harry, when he has learned that Harry and Valentia are closer than cousins. Through the minds of other characters, our knowledge of Harry is increased, but it must always be censored by what we know of them: "Valentia often said that Romer should never do more than walk through a room or look in for a few minutes where there were other people—even at a club—and then go away immediately, when he would leave a striking impression. If he stayed longer he became alarming. His personality was so extraordinarily *nil* that it was quite oppressive" (14).

This attitude compares to the reaction of Romer's mother, who is a quick-witted and quick-tempered woman: "She adored Romer, although his slow speech and long pauses often drove her to the very verge of violence" (38). The contrast between Harry and Romer is complete, and is made explicit by sentences like "He [Harry] had . . . a genius for love-making, but he had not, like Romer, a genius for love" (107). Romer is silent and patient where Harry is voluble and volatile. Like Felicity Chetwode's flirtation with Bertie Wilton in *The Twelfth Hour,* Valentia's attraction to Harry is caused or increased by the similarity of their temperaments.

Various friends and relatives warn all three members of the triangle. Mrs. Wyburn, Romer's mother, admires and deplores her daughter-in-law, loves her son, and adores malice. Valentia knows what her mother-in-law thinks of her: "She says I'm frivolous and worldly and an utter fool and very deep . . ." (19); and hers is not a bad summary. Mrs. Wyburn is much less bland than most of Mrs. Leverson's other dowagers: "She always wore a hard-looking black silk dress. She had parted black hair, long ear-rings, and a knot of rare old imitation lace at her throat. Eagerness, impatience, love of teasing and sharp wit were visible in her face to one who could read between the lines" (37).

One of the best passages in the novel is a gossip between Mrs. Wyburn and her confidante, Miss Westbury; the conversation begins tranquilly, with Miss Westbury leaning back in her chair "with the comfortable amiability of a fat woman who expects to be amused" (170); but it quickly moves into high gear:

> "I doubt if my son is happy."
> "Oh, really, really? Do you think he's *ever noticed anything?* Isn't he devoted to Harry de Freyne?"
> "Of course he hates him like poison," replied the mother.
> Miss Westbury started in delighted horror, and replied sharply, "How do you know that? Did he tell you?"
> "Tell me! He would never tell me. Besides, he couldn't tell me—he doesn't know it."
> "And how do you know it?"
> "Mothers know everything," she replied. (174–75)

Earlier Miss Westbury has sharpened Mrs. Wyburn's suspicions by reporting that their friend Jane Totness had seen Valentia and Harry together in the British Museum; and, as Miss Westbury says, "Who on earth would go to the British Museum, unless they were dragged there by force, except to have a private interview?" (93).

The war between Valentia and Mrs. Wyburn is the classic one between wife and mother-in-law. Mrs. Leverson gives one dangerous little scene between them. Listening to Valentia, Mrs. Wyburn "admired her pluck and the fit of her dress" (125); they are evenly matched:

> "What *delicious* China tea! Yours is the only house where one gets it quite like this."
> She put down her cup, which was more than half full, with a slight sigh.
> "Romer hates China tea too," said Mrs. Wyburn. "It would be really better for your nerves if you'd drink it, my dear." (125)

Despite the warnings that Valentia and Harry receive, they are busy devising plans to ensure the continuance of their relationship. They wish to marry Daphne, Valentia's younger sister who lives with her, to an American millionaire, Matthew Van Buren, to get her out of the way, and they work assiduously toward that end. But Daphne does not fall in with the plan. Graver damage is done to Valentia's hopes by the discovery that Harry, deeply in debt, has a private scheme, which is to marry the immensely rich young Alec Walmer. Alec is a slangy, athletic, and pathetic girl, "who at the first glance looked eight feet high, but who really was not very much above the average length" (51); she is the daughter of the completely cynical Lady Walmer, "a faded yet powerful beauty" whom even royalty had found interesting: which has an irony of its own, since Alec is named after her "distinguished godmother" Princess Alexandra, wife of Edward.

Yet the dénouement is not the result of Harry's perfidy. Romer overhears a conversation between his wife and her cousin which discloses the depth of their attachment and Valentia's grief at Harry's plan to marry an heiress. His chief accusation against Harry in a scene between them shows the single-mindedness of his love for his wife: "And *you* made her cry. You! You made her cry!" (283). He forces Harry to write a letter breaking his engagement to Alec; and, although Romer has impulses to murder Harry, he at first plans to let the *ménage à trois* continue as before so that Valentia will not be deprived of Harry. But jealousy overwhelms him; he reaches "the limit of his endurance" (289); and he decides to tell Harry to leave permanently. Before this can happen, Harry, marveling at Romer's simplicity, tells Valentia of the scene between the two men and of Romer's self-sacrifice. In a revulsion of feeling Valentia recognizes her husband's generosity and love and sends Harry away.

If Valentia were merely the victim of passion, we would hesitate to condemn her. But the passion brings with it a train of unattractive and unresisted attitudes and deeds. In her insistence on finding a rich husband for Daphne, practicality has passed into cynicism; and, worse, it ignores Daphne's love for a young Guards officer, Cyril Foster. She is equally wrong in manipulating Daphne's life and her husband's; the masterly persiflage with which she can persuade Romer not to accompany her to a dinner party at Harry's can, in colder terms, be called cruel. Her egoism is also unpleasant; in her drawing room is the portrait Harry did of her, and her love for her sister, who, she thinks, is "almost as pretty as herself" (21), derives in part from her belief that Daphne's looks complement her own. Her callousness toward Romer is shown by the carelessness with which she betrays herself several times in conversation: "Why, Lady Walmer would be quite as dangerous a rival for me as a woman ten years or twenty years younger" (121). Worst of all, her return to Romer at the end of the novel is marked by no admission of guilt on her part. She learns that Romer loves her better, not that she has behaved cruelly to him. Mrs. Leverson succeeds in establishing Valentia's fascination, but not that she has a heart.

That the liaison with Harry was sexual has been assumed by some critics, but the matter is debatable. Mrs. Leverson speaks of Valentia and Harry's "romance," a noncommittal term. The first time they are alone together, Harry sounds silly enough to be a lover: "How interesting you are! One of your eyebrows is thicker than the other" (29). Valentia's jealousy of Alec and Lady Walmer, and Harry's of Romer and Hereford Vaughan (jealousy plays as indefatigable a part in the lives of these characters as it does in the preceding novels), at times sounds sexual in nature. But jealousy often does; and against such evidence is the conventionality of Valentia. It is not a question of Edwardian proprieties—Mrs. Leverson was to include a seduction (though offstage) in her next novel—but rather that it is not basically relevant. In a novel of today we expect sex, and we expect it to be graphic; but such was not the case in 1911. In any intelligent terms, Edwardian or contemporary, Valentia's guilt is established whether she met Harry in the garden at dawn to take snapshots (224) or for other purposes. Mrs. Leverson may have wished to hint, she may have wished to be ambiguous, she may not have decided: just as she had not decided about the moral character of Valentia, and did not know that she had not.

## III *Potpourri*

The story of Valentia, Romer, and Harry is the center of *The Limit,* but there are so many loose ends and extraneous characters that the triangle does not hold the novel together. The book could be called *Sketches of London Life.* The most episodic and diffuse of the six novels, *The Limit* is a kind of permissive writing, where the author relinquishes esthetic control and allows her penchants for oddity, joke, and personal reference to control her. In *Love's Shadow,* the preceding novel, there is a brief mention of an 1890's survival, a poet named Hazel Kerr who "came here the other day and brought with him a poem in bronze lacquer, as he called it. He read it aloud—the whole of it" (22). But in *The Limit,* in the scene where Harry meets Valentia at dawn in the garden, there are actual phrases from letters of Wilde to the Sphinx: Harry calls Valentia a "minion of the moon' as Wilde called Mrs. Leverson; and when Harry says, "I knew you had clothes for every possible occasion; but still, to choose the exact right dress to put on to meet your cousin at dawn in the orchard . . ." (231), he is echoing Wilde's remark to Mrs. Leverson when she met him at seven o'clock on the morning after he was released from prison.[18]

The novel contains a Henry James anecdote (215–16); a puff for her friend Reggie Turner's novel *Count Florio and Phillis K.* (263); and a good deal of dialect humor from Mrs. Mills, Hereford Vaughan's housekeeper (191–92), as well as from the innkeeper's daughter, Gladys Brill, whom Vaughan briefly fancies (241–42 and elsewhere). The slang of Alec Walmer ("You *are* a rotter, Harry!," "*How* much?'," and so on, 141–43) is funnier. Vaughan's cheery confidant, Muir Howard, serves no other function in the novel except to make Matthew Van Buren, the American millionaire, briefly jealous by his attentions to Daphne. Daphne visits Mrs. Foster, the mother of the "baby Guardsman" she is engaged to; and Mrs. Foster, a demure old lady, reads aloud to Daphne poems she has written in her youth when she was "very much under the influence of the Passionate School—Swinburne, Rossetti, Ella Wheeler Wilcox, and so on . . ." (152). One called "Night Time" begins:

> He glanced as he passed,
> And I hope, and I quiver,
> I howl and I shudder with pains;
> And like a she-tiger
> Or overcharged river,
> My blood rushes on through my veins. (153)

But the question of whether or not Daphne is ever to marry Cyril Foster is left hanging in the air. It is interesting that Daphne, early an orphan, has a mother fixation on Mrs. Foster, who feeds her gingerbread nuts and good advice, but such observations become peripheral when we do not learn what happens to Daphne.

Certain other minor characters are relevant to the central action to greater or less degree, although we never feel that the plot would suffer from their absence. The millionaire Van Buren briefly admires Daphne and serves as Harry's confidant; for, among Harry's other vices, he is one of those men who no sooner kisses than he hastens to tell; and at the end of the novel Harry's future is assured, as if we cared, by his accompanying Van Buren to New York where he will be employed in the American's bank. Intrinsically, however, Van Buren's interest is that of caricature: "He had very broad shoulders, and a very thin waist, and that naïve worldliness of air so captivating in many of his countrymen" (33). In contrast to Harry's cynicism, Van Buren has "sensitive delicate feelings" and a "high standard of morals with regard to what he called the ladies, and illusions that one would rarely find in London in a girl of seventeen . . ." (49). As Harry says of him, "He always gets rather excited in the evening after dinner and so much Perrier water . . ." (27–28). Van Buren may have been intended as moral foil, but anyone who speaks of a "ro-mance" with a "broonette" (113, 33) can be taken no more seriously than his English friends take him.

Hereford Vaughan, the playwright who has eleven plays running simultaneously "in American, in Eskimo, and even in Turkish, besides in every known European language" (183), twice warns Valentia (193, 225); but much more space is given to his wooing of Gladys Brill, daughter of the proprietor of the "Bald-faced Stag" at Edgware. Impulsively he proposes: "He thought of Harry de Freyne, and felt noble and superior in contrast to what *his* conduct would have been . . ." (259), only to learn that Gladys has long been engaged to the son of a neighboring pub-keeper. Some early reviewers found both Matthew Van Buren and Gladys Brill natural and lifelike; today they seem caricatures, figures from feuilletons or comic operettas.

Much the best of the minor figures, and one of Mrs. Leverson's splendid comic creations, is the actress Flora Luscombe. Her connection with Valentia, Romer, and Harry is tenuous at best; once, having tea in the Carlton with the stagestruck, tattooed gentleman, Mr. Rathbone, she sees a tête-à-tête between Valentia and Harry; but the incident leads to nothing. Miss

Luscombe needs no function; she exists. Based upon Aubrey Beardsley's sister Mabel, to whom Yeats wrote poems and of whom Max Beerbohm said he could not overstate her strange charm,[19] Flora's failure as an actress may be due to the fact that "on the stage they think she's in society, and in society they believe she's on the stage" (27).

At times, Flora is nothing but affectations, as when she attends a dinner party: "She pouted childishly, gave her arch musical laugh with its three soprano notes and upward inflection, and then accepted a quail with a heavy sigh" (56). She lives in a semi-basement flat, which her acquaintances call "the tank," with her mother, who "was so refined that there was scarcely anything of her; her presence was barely perceptible" (82); but Mrs. Luscombe can be irascible enough when Flora becomes too kittenish. Flora is highly social and is fond of entertaining in "the tank": "The Luscombes lived, as it were, beneath the surface; but that did not prevent their being very much *dans le mouvement,* and coming up with great frequency to the surface to breathe" (79). Even when she is by herself, Flora does not become natural: "She always hummed a little tune when she was alone, if possible some quaint old French air" (131). When she has her poor mother as captive audience, she is uncontrollable:

> Flora laughed coquettishly, putting on her Russian Princess manner. It was voluble, disdainful, and condescending. She often changed, quite suddenly, from an *ingénue* to a *grande dame,* and then to an adventuress and back again before you knew where you were.
>
> . . . Miss Luscombe now became a soubrette of a somewhat hooligan type, and pretended to throw a little feather duster she was holding into the depths of the arm-chair. (132–33)

Mrs. Leverson knows Flora so thoroughly that she can add detail after detail to the characterization; for example, of Flora's hand, she writes, "It was a pretty hand, thin and bony, with pink polished nails and a garnet ring . . ." (136). But the most expert touches are those which reveal the human being beneath Flora's fanciful manner and elevate her beyond caricature. When Rathbone finally proposes marriage to her, she can not at first believe him:

> "Are you making fun of me?" she asked, in a trembling voice, "because that would not be right. It wouldn't be nice of you—in fact, it would be rather cruel."

"You don't mean to say you care for me the least little bit?" He took both her hands and stared hard at her face. "Is there something real about you then?" he continued.

Tears came to her eyes. She turned her head away.

There is indeed "something real" about Flora; and after St. George's, Hanover Square, they go to Oberammergau for their honeymoon.

Flora disappears a little more than halfway through the book; at this point, the romance of Hereford Vaughan with Gladys Brill begins. If the story of Vaughan and Gladys had been finished too soon, we feel that Mrs. Leverson would cheerfully have furnished a third and fourth romantic subplot. In *The Limit,* she fills up her three hundred allotted pages willy-nilly; it is more like the series of sketches for a novel than a finished and polished work.

## IV *Insights*

Whatever its faults, *The Limit* has, with Flora and Mrs. Wyburn and Van Buren, with Mrs. Leverson's own comments and jokes and situations, comedy, humor, and wit. And it has, more frequently than the other novels, its wisdom, where the comedy is momentarily abandoned for what Inez Holden called a "secondary sadness" and for what Adrian Alington labeled the "deeper side" of Mrs. Leverson's talent. In their sudden intelligence and exactitude these moments, whenever they occur in the novels, lift us out of the theater into a different pleasure—that of life observations which have become life lessons.

In *Love's Shadow,* at the time Hyacinth believes that her husband has not abandoned his former love, Mrs. Leverson injects, "As a rule the person found out in a betrayal of love holds . . . the superior position of the two. It is the betrayed one who is humiliated" (302). In *The Limit* also, love often prompts the striking generalization. For example, Romer, though Valentia may be dishonest with him, wishes only to keep her as his wife: "It never even occurred to him to try to act as the husband ought to act, or as by the incessant insidious influence of plays and novels most of us have been brought up to think he ought to act. Most people are far more guided than they know in their views of life by the artificial conventions of the theatre and of literature, or by tradition. In fact, most people are other people. Romer was himself" (284).

Of marriage, and of male and female intuition, she writes: "The marvellous instinct with which women are usually credited seems too often to desert them on the only occasions when it would be of any real use. One would say it was there for trivialities only, since in a crisis they are usually dense, fatally doing the wrong thing. It is hardly too much to say that most domestic tragedies are caused by the feminine intuition of men and the want of it in women" (300).

Of friendship, she remarks, after making clear that Hereford Vaughan is both bored and irritated with his friend Muir Howard, "There is always something agreeable in a habit of which one is a little tired" (186). She can seize upon a particular situation and use it both to illuminate the character concerned and character in general; here is Mrs. Wyburn, tediously embroidering elaborate buttonholes: "She had that decadent love of minute finish in the unessential so often seen in persons of a nervous yet persistent temperament" (123). And still more damagingly, she comments on Harry's friendship with Matthew Van Buren, "It was his nature to make use of everything. It is an infallible sign of the second-rate in nature and intellect to make use of everything and of every one. The genius is incapable of making use of people. It is for the second-rate clever people to make use of him" (108). *The Limit* is a flimsy novel, but not in such probings of experience as these.

## CHAPTER 8

# Tenterhooks

### I *Love at First Sight*

LOVE'S *Shadow,* Mrs. Leverson's second novel and the first of the three "little Ottley" novels, is an advance on her first work, *The Twelfth Hour;* and *Tenterhooks,* her fourth novel, published in 1912, and the second of the Ottley novels, is superior to its predecessor, *The Limit,* although, as with *The Twelfth Hour* and *Love's Shadow,* only one year separates the publication dates of the two works. *Tenterhooks* is not a sequel to *Love's Shadow,* despite the reappearance of Bruce and Edith Ottley. Earlier they were subordinate characters; now they are the center of the stage, and they occupy that position throughout, thereby supplying the novel with the strong focus and development that *The Limit* conspicuously lacks.

In *Tenterhooks,* when we again meet Edith and Bruce Ottley, Bruce is the same boor as before, but Edith has changed. Not only is she now twenty-eight and a mature woman, having outgrown those touches of girlishness we saw in *Love's Shadow;* but she has come into her own in other ways. Chief of these is that she has taken command of her marriage and now has an unshakable sense of her own dignity and worth. She has been too kind in having been "endlessly patient" with Bruce: patience, good nature, and understanding are powerful weapons, not for those who exercise them, but those upon whom they are exercised. Edith has not become a Valentia Wyburn, cynically manipulating her husband; her tact and forbearance survive. But at times she asserts herself. Self-assertion may work no better than patient self-suppression because Bruce is as insensitive to one as to the other; but if her self-assertion does Bruce no good, it clearly benefits Edith: it is one of those safe aggression patterns that behaviorist psychologists recommend.

The opening pages of the novel show Edith's daily life, a prelude to the event that is dramatically to change her life—the introduction to Aylmer Ross. The firmer, more forthright way in which she counters Bruce's frailties is demonstrated several times, as, for example, when he tiresomely explains his presentiment that they would not attend the Mitchells' dinner party (the fact is that he gets both the date and the address wrong):

". . . I often think I'm a pessimist, yet look how well I'm taking it. I'm more like a fatalist—sometimes I hardly know what I am."

"I could tell you what you are," said Edith, "but I won't. . . ." (20)

At a later dinner party of the Mitchells, she meets the forty-year-old barrister who is to be the love of her life, and one result is that her grievances against Bruce become outspoken, although she knows why only subconsciously. In one of the longest speeches in the novel—and it sounds a little like a speech—she states her complaints fully:

. . . We've been married eight years; you leave the housekeeping, the whole ordering of the children's education, and heaps of other quite important things, entirely to me; in fact, you lead almost the life of a schoolboy, without any of the tiresome part, and with freedom, going to school in the day and amusing yourself in the evening, while everything disagreeable and important is thought of and seen to for you. You only have the children with you when they amuse you. *I* have all the responsibility; I have to be patient, thoughtful—in fact, you leave things to me more than most men do to their wives, Bruce. You won't be bothered even to look at an account—to do a thing. But I'm not complaining. (135–36)

Bruce's rejoinder—"Oh, you're not! It sounded a little like it" —can, after Edith's perfectly just but relentless harangue, make us rather like him. However, throughout most of *Tenterhooks* he is as much a monster as ever. In the following passage he wishes to cancel an invitation to a dinner party at his mother's for a more interesting engagement:

"Won't your mother be disappointed?" Edith asked.

"My dear Edith, you can safely leave that to me. Of course she'll be disappointed, but you can go round and see her, and speak to her nicely and tell her that after all we can't come because we've got another engagement."

"And am I to tell her it's a subsequent one? Otherwise she'll wonder we didn't mention it before."

"Don't be in a hurry, dear. Don't rush things; remember . . . she's my mother. Perhaps to you, Edith, it seems a rather old-fashioned idea, and I daresay you think it's rot, but to me there's something very sacred about the idea of a mother." He lit a cigarette and looked in the glass. (82)

It is typical of Bruce that, in the prologue of the novel, when Edith is giving birth to their second child, he should be in Carlsbad, taking the cure for (a probably imaginary) rheumatism.

Edith, however, before meeting Aylmer Ross, is shown coping successfully with Bruce and with everything. She shines particularly as a mother, and there are charmingly unsentimental scenes of her in the nursery with her two children, Archie, who is six, and Dilly, who is four. One misses Mrs. Leversons' humorous knowledge of children in *The Limit,* the only one of the six novels with an entirely adult cast.

Aylmer is everything that Bruce is not—intellectual, witty, sophisticated and mature. Bruce is "incapable of caring for any woman (however feebly) for more than two or three weeks" and is "particularly fickle, vague, and scrappy in his emotions" (205); but the widower Aylmer falls in love with Edith at once, "a rare and genuine case of *coup de foudre*" (72). Herself highly attracted, Edith is finally impelled fully into love with Aylmer by, as might be predicted from the earlier novels, jealousy. As might also be predicted, it is by chance that she sees Aylmer driving with a young art student—who we know from the beginning, however, can be no real threat to Edith because she has the ridiculous name of Mavis Argles.

But Mavis, with her "pretty, weary, dreary, young, blue eyes" (142), causes trouble. She is very poor; and for some time has been the mistress of Vincy, Edith's special confidant. Vincy, whose full name is Vincy Wenham Vincy, is an esthete, witty, discreet, much more the observer than the actor, and fond of speaking Cockney. He is modeled after Reggie Turner, Mrs. Leverson's friend; Max Beerbohm, another friend, thought *Tenterhooks* "delightful . . . especially the Reggie Turner in it."[1] Despite his sympathy for Mavis' poverty and her physical attractiveness to him, Vincy feels that there is "something false, worrying, unreliable and incalculable" in her and eludes her demand that he marry her.

If Mavis cannot have an unmarried man, she will settle for a married one. Bruce, earlier caught by Edith in a flirtation with the children's governess, is only too ready to oblige; and when Mavis believes or pretends to believe she is pregnant, Bruce writes a ridiculous farewell letter to Edith, which includes the sentence "Mavis Argles and I are all in all to each other"; and then Mavis and Bruce elope to Australia.

This event precipitates the moral climax of the novel. Aylmer is desperate for Edith to divorce Bruce and marry him, but she refuses. For the sake of her children, and for the sake of Bruce, whom she pities, and for other less clear but high-minded motives, she allows Bruce to return, no questions asked; and he quickly does so. On shipboard, Mavis and he had quarreled; he (or they) learned that she was not pregnant; and Mavis had acquired a new protector, whom she married on arrival in Australia. Frustrated beyond endurance, Aylmer leaves Edith; and the last chapter in the novel contains another domestic scene like those which began the novel—Bruce complains once again that the inkwell is too full, and he remarks that he is "a bit sunburnt" from his voyage.

## II *An Ideal Woman*

To catalogue the virtues of the Edith Ottley of *Tenterhooks* is to summarize the novel. Each of her attractions interestingly contains a contradiction which increases it; for example, though she is beautiful, her beauty is quiet, not flamboyant. She has a "sure impressionistic gift" for dress, but she is "not even much interested" in clothing. "Always an immense favourite with women," she "frankly preferred the society of the average man." She has no taste for coquetry, but has "many natural gifts" for it (32–33). And, when she is less than perfect, her defects are of the type of which Mrs. Leverson intends us to say, "How human." Although Edith is "the most reposeful woman in London" (102), she can rouse herself to righteous anger with the governess who had flirted with Bruce and congratulate herself on Bruce's momentary contrition: "Edith was really delighted, she felt she had won, and she *did* want that horrid little Townsend to be scored off! Wasn't it natural?" (188). She loses the self-control she prides herself on ("Edith had a high opinion of her own strength of will" [168]) when she sees Aylmer with Mavis Argles, and piqued, she writes him a furious note (174).

Quite minor, but quite unforgivable, is Edith's treatment of her faithful friend Miss Bennett, who does shopping for her; her greeting to Miss Bennett in one scene is, "rather reproachfully," "You're late, Grace" (99); the scene and chapter end, after Grace has run through London like a hare on Edith's errands, "With a quiet smile, Edith dismissed her" (105). Not at all minor is the way Edith forgives poor Bruce for Miss Townsend and Miss Argles but never for a moment questions her own deception of him with Aylmer: she is Aylmer's mistress in everything but physical fact. Her duplicity is serenely unselfconscious.

But these are the prerogatives of a heroine. That Edith is a dominant and vivid creation, or that she has a heroine's true authority, is shown by the way she has irritated critics:

> Edith Ottley is a good-looking, commonplace, stupid woman, without depth or passion: and I very much fear that the author, who has become infatuated with her, does not see this.[2]
>
> . . .
>
> The author is so unaffectedly on Edith's side throughout the Ottleys' matrimonial troubles, and Bruce is allowed so few marks (his successes with women are always discounted, and it is more than once explained that in spite of his behaviour he was really in love with his wife), that in the end Bruce almost wins the reader's sympathy. Was it perhaps Edith who was really the difficult one?[3]

The first description of Edith is inaccurate, and the second treats her as if she were real not fictional; but both show how she compels reaction, debate, speculation. Aylmer is nearly as idealized a man as Edith is a woman: "He was the sort of man who is adored by children, animals, servants and women. Tall, strong and handsome, with intelligence beyond the average, yet with nothing alarming about him, good-humoured about trifles, jealous in matters of love . . ." (69). He is romantic, and falls in love at first sight. He is passionate: "Not one man in a thousand was capable of feeling so intensely and deeply as Aylmer felt

. . ." (163). He is virile: "I'm not a man who could ever be a tame cat" (109). He embodies the antimaterialism of the materialistic Edwardians (that same lip-service paid in America today): "He had no pleasure in property; valuable possessions worried him . . . he really liked money only for freedom and ease" (71). He is no more honest than Edith in his treatment of Bruce, for he acts the role of close friend and good companion when his real opinion of Bruce is "*'Il n'a qu'un défaut—il est impossible'*" (165).

Aylmer is defeated by Edith, and he storms out of the novel in a passion of rage and love. Like Charlotte Brontë's *Jane Eyre, Tenterhooks* can be read as a document of female supremacy. Edith has human lapses, but she is at her worst as implacably superior as Sophocles' Antigone. It is characteristic of her that she is opposed to the suffragette movement (135): she does not want a man's rights; she wants a woman's rights, and reckons them largely. We wonder how many first nights of Ibsen's plays Mrs. Leverson attended, for Edith is in many ways like Ibsen's Nora, Hedda, and Mrs. Alving.

## III *From Dramatist to Novelist*

The habit of writing in short scenes of quasi-dramatic nature was ingrained in Mrs. Leverson by her long experience as a journalist and by her love of the theater, yet *Tenterhooks* is more like a conventional novel than the three books it followed. It still is episodic, and has the quick pace which is attractive in everything she wrote; but it adds certain dimensions. For example, like many another novel, it concerns a moral choice. Unfortunately, Edith's need for a choice does not rise to the status of dilemma: she too automatically rules out adultery, never considering, with the intelligent reflection of which she is capable, the immorality of marriage to a totally unsuited man. The moral context would engage us more if Edith faltered even to the extent that Valentia Wyburn, a less intelligent woman, does. But then, Mrs. Leverson was "at bottom a good Victorian," as someone once wrote of her.[4]

The plot of *Tenterhooks,* Mrs. Leverson's shortest novel, is Mrs. Leverson's strongest and simplest plot so far. It is a love story. In earlier novels her only plot principle was a happy eclecticism, and she abandoned her main characters when someone or something else temporarily amused her more. But here the structure dominates. Edith meets Aylmer; he leaves her twice, both times because he cannot be a "tame cat." The first time is temporary: he returns, summoned back by her from Paris; the second time he leaves for permanent exile from her, since, given reason to divorce Bruce, she did not; therefore family and marriage win.

Also, though *Tenterhooks* is a dialogue novel, its dependence on dialogue is to a significant degree supplanted by an exploration of mental processes. We are inside Edith's and Aylmer's minds much oftener, and for longer, than in those of characters in the three earlier novels, and the state of their emotions is described with much patient and careful detail. Colin MacInnes is so impressed by the psychology that he writes that "Love's agony, and jealousy, and pain in joy are present in *Tenterhooks* to such effect that those who, being in love, may read it, had better not, and those who have been, but are not now, will sharply be reminded of what they may think they have forgotten. The temperature of emotions rises steadily in the book until it stands unbearably . . . at its fever heat."[5] *Tenterhooks* is the only one of the six Leverson novels that ends unhappily. An item in George Moore's literary esthetic was the principle of "eternal recurrence," where the ending of a novel repeats the beginning, a repetition that emphasizes how much has changed between. In *Tenterhooks*, we are treated to Bruce's boorish insensitivity at the end as we were at the beginning, and we see with a deep sense of irony that things are the same—Bruce is still Bruce—but also different: Edith has met Aylmer, loved him, and let him go.

An ordinary literary tool like irony is common to drama and fiction, and Mrs. Leverson's other works make copious use of it; yet the distancing effect of irony in *Tenterhooks* is like that of novels, suggestive and expansive, rather than like that of dramas, where it tends to be used for immediate point. Just before Edith sees Bruce with the governess in the park, we are told, "She was reminding herself she must be gentle, good, to Bruce. He had at least never deceived her!" (183). Any situation involving Mavis Argles has an ironic level to it, whether it is Vincy, telling Edith that he wishes he could get "some nice person to . . . take her [Mavis] on" (210)—which is what Bruce is just about to do, unknown to either Vincy or Edith. Elsewhere Bruce, in the throes of sympathy for Mavis, despises the anonymous "fiend" who had "thrown her over" and meets Vincy immediately after these thoughts with a warmly affectionate greeting. The irony in *Tenterhooks* has enlarged from epigram to situation; it is integral, not arbitrary.

## IV *Unhappy Endings*

The vision of *Tenterhooks* is darker, though there are still jokes, comic characters, epigrams. Lady Everard, who is a plump comic widow who "never stopped talking for a single moment, but in a way that resembled leaking rather than laying down the law" (86), and who is highly interested in music and young male musicians, though perhaps not in that order, is another in Mrs. Leverson's gallery of dowagers. Vincy has "a gift of reading people's minds," and Mrs. Leverson, remarking how people never object to his gift, says, "Most people would far rather be seen through than not be seen at all" (265). And a time or two we meet the highly inarticulate but persistent Captain Willis, who can say "in a confidential tone" to his dinner partner, "Do you know, what I always say is—live and let live and let it go at that; what?" (47).

But the story itself in its serious sadness outweighs such comic interludes as these. The culminating irony is Edith's rejection of an ideal man for a man whom eight years have shown to be the opposite. Near the end of the novel, Vincy urges Edith to abandon Bruce to Mavis, divorce him, and marry Aylmer:

> ". . . Everything would be all nicely settled up, just like the fourth act of a play. And *then* I should be glad I hadn't married Mavis. . . . Oh, do let it be like the fourth act, Edith."
>
> "How can life be like a play? It's hopeless to attempt it," she said rather sadly. (267)

And another example of the sobering realism of Edith at her most intelligent is her reply to Aylmer when he, in despair at her willingness to take Bruce back, asks her if she thinks that Bruce will be a better man and husband after his Mavis escapade: " 'Do people alter?' she answered" (273).

It is easy, but essentially irrelevant, to read into Edith's marriage the story of Mrs. Leverson's own marriage or into Edith's probity Mrs. Leverson's justification of herself as woman and as wife. *Tenterhooks* needs no such adventitious interest, for it substantiates its own darker vision by its strong, plain plot; by its characters and their explored relations with one another; and by the irony which objectifies and generalizes these explorations and makes them a believably possible part of any reader's experience.

## CHAPTER 9

# Bird of Paradise

### I *Echoes*

"I should like to burn you, like spice, on the altar of a devoted friendship" (95). In a letter to Madeline Irwin, Rupert Denison of *Bird of Paradise,* who is another of those 1890's figures like Vincy in *Tenterhooks,* writes this singular sentence. Rupert, with his boutonniere of violets matching his violet socks (50), is actually quoting a sentence that Mrs. Leverson used in one of her *Punch* contributions in 1896.[1] And when Nigel Hillier calls Bertha Kellynch a "minion of the moon" (35), he is not only repeating what Harry de Freyne called Valentia Wyburn in *The Limit* (231) but is returning to Wilde himself, who used the phrase for the Sphinx.[2] On another occasion Wilde wrote to the Sphinx that she was "one of those—alas, too few—who are always followed by the flutes of the Pagan World";[3] Rupert uses these identical words about Bertha Kellynch in *Bird of Paradise,* written over twenty years later; and Stanley Wilson writes them in a letter to his mistress in "The Blow," the story which appeared in the *English Review,* six years later.

*Bird of Paradise,* the fifth of Mrs. Leverson's six novels, which was published in 1914, is full of such echoes. We understand her treasuring of Wilde's words, but the recall of fragments of very minor sketches written many years before—and every one of her six novels repeats such odds and ends—is startling. It is a sign of the limitations of her inventiveness, and of her loyalties and the consistency of her outlook in that, once she had used a line or phrase, or (more rarely) a character or situation, she was apt to reuse it. Her imagination operated on varying the prototype.

Thus there are again a dowager (Lady Kellynch), a schoolboy (Clifford Kellynch), a would-be lover (Nigel Hillier)—who has, exactly like Bertie Wilton in *The Twelfth Hour* of seven years earlier, "the most mischievous smile in London" (34). But none of these characters is identical with his or her predecessors; like William Congreve or I. Compton-Burnett, two other masters of the comedy of manners, Mrs. Leverson uses types; and like them, she varies the type from comedy to comedy.

Bertha Kellynch, the heroine of *Bird of Paradise,* is as pretty as Mrs. Leverson's other heroines, but quite different in appearance. She is like a canary, small, plump, and blonde. Her husband Percy is "a rather serious-looking barrister with parliamentary ambitions, . . . a fine forehead, behind which there was less doing than one would suppose, polished manners, an amiable disposition and private means" (14); and he has continued during his ten years of marriage to Bertha "to regard her as a pet and a luxury" (40). He has allowed her to decorate their house as she pleases, "rather in the same way that one would give an intelligent canary *carte blanche* about the decoration of what was supposed to be its cage" (14).

But Bertha is not so brainless as a canary; she is highly intelligent, highly observant, and good and likable. She wears her rectitude much more lightly than the Edith Ottley of *Tenterhooks,* and is like Felicity Chetwode or Valentia Wyburn in her gay charm; but she is less frivolous than the former and lacks the cynicism of the latter. Bertha's problem is one met with earlier—it is especially the problem of Felicity among earlier heroines: "I've always had a sort of ideal or dream of making an ordinary married life into a romance" (99). The solution, as any one of the four earlier novels would also suggest, is the awakening of jealousy—though not, of course, by means of conscious strategem.

At the age of eighteen Bertha, who is now twenty-eight, was in love with Nigel Hillier. Nigel resembles Harry de Freyne in *The Limit* in his dedication to the art of love, in his animation and energy, in his caddishness; Nigel is, however, more intelligent and less self-loving than Harry, more of a man, but harder. Both Bertha and Nigel were poor (in the way that upper-class people can be poor); but, where Bertha was content to wait, Nigel wasn't. He married a red-haired heiress, only, ironically, to be left a legacy a few months after his marriage (in the way that upper-class people, at least in novels, can be left legacies): a legacy that would have made marriage to Bertha possible. In the meantime Bertha, cured of her love for Nigel, has fallen in love with Percy, married him, and become his canary.

Nigel's wife Mary has become a jealous tyrant. She is right in suspecting that Nigel is still in love with Bertha, or even more so —because of the impossibility of fulfillment—than he was ten years ago; but Mary is wrong in suspecting that Bertha returns his interest. Bertha remains deeply in love with her husband, who is a somewhat livelier type than the silent Romer of *The Limit,* and she barely tolerates Nigel's visits. The pretext for these visits is Madeline Irwin, Bertha's closest friend, who has two suitors, Rupert Denison and Charlie Hillier, Nigel's younger brother. Nigel helps Bertha plot Madeline's capture of Rupert, whose schoolmaster qualities Madeline finds overwhelmingly attractive: "I'm sure I don't want all these silly dancing young men. They bore me to death. Give me *culture!* and all that sort of thing" (14). In contrast to earlier young "second leads" in the novels like Sylvia Crofton in *The Twelfth Hour* or Daphne de Freyne in *The Limit,* who are rather flat portraits, Madeline is well realized. She has the foolishness of youth but is mature enough to know that her rapturous love for the suave Rupert is the real thing.

Rupert is—not torn, he is too immaculate to be torn—but divided between his interest in Madeline, whose sensitivity and worship he enjoys patronizing, and in Moona Chivvey, an untalented art student of coarse high spirits. Temporarily neglecting Madeline for Moona, Rupert ends by finding Moona too saucy and unmanageable; and he proposes to the gentle and teachable Madeline. But Madeline, through Nigel's machinations and because she has lost hope of winning Rupert, has been proposed to in the meantime by Charlie Hillier at a tango tea and has accepted him. When Madeline receives a letter from Rupert asking her to marry him, she hastily breaks the engagement with Charlie, only to find that Rupert, deeply offended at her act of independence in accepting Charlie, counsels her to marry Charlie and then departs for the Continent.

When Madeline has been deserted, her mother's very amusing concern adds to Madeline's unhappy discomfiture. Mrs. Irwin has "all the Victorian desire to see her daughter married young, and all the Victorian almost absurd delicacy in pretending she didn't" (194). "Mrs. Irwin was a woman who detested facts, so much so that she thought statistics positively indecent (though she would never have used the expression). When she was told there were more women than men in England, she would bite her lips and change the subject" (193–94). At the moment when Madeline has accepted Charlie and receives Rupert's letter of proposal, Mrs. Irwin could "only regret bitterly that Madeline could not accept them both, it being very rare nowadays for two agreeable and eligible young men to propose to one girl in two days" (170). In the end, Rupert again proposes, and Madeline accepts. Their marriage will undoubtedly be a happy if somewhat bookish one, for Madeline will ever strive to attain the "*culture!*" her husband represents.

Mary Hillier is not concerned with Madeline, only with what she suspects is her husband's affair with Bertha. She writes a series of anonymous letters to Percy, who becomes jealous; and, though saying nothing of the letters, he urges Bertha to drop Nigel. Flattered by his jealousy, she consents. However, she is pressed by Nigel to attend a large party Mary is giving; and, herself reluctant, and with Percy's reluctant consent, she arrives at the party to be met with Mary's violent, and to Bertha inexplicable, abuse: "If you don't make that woman go away at once, I shall make a public scene!" (201). Bertha leaves of her own accord and does not tell Percy of the incident, just as he had not told her of the letters. A final anonymous letter causes him to confront Nigel with it and its predecessors and order him to cease his attentions to Bertha. Knowing that Mary has written the letters, Nigel pities her—"With the weak good nature that was in Nigel, curiously side by side with a certain cruel hardness, he now felt a little sorry for her" (250)—and punishes her after she admits her guilt by separating from her for some weeks. With Bertha now lost to him permanently, he meets Moona Chivvey by chance in Paris, and he flirts with her unsatisfactorily for an evening or two. One big item in his chagrin is not only that it is now clear that Bertha and Percy (who has promoted his wife ornithologically from canary to bird of paradise) are unshakably in love but also that, sign and testament to the love, Bertha is to become a mother, as for ten years she has longed to be.

Yet though Nigel is a weak man, the course of his own marriage improves. During his absence, Mary visits Bertha for advice, which Bertha sympathetically gives: don't nag, be cheerful, love your children, and so forth. The advice works, and Mrs. Leverson writes, "I find I am finishing my story in a manner no less strange than unconventional nowadays: I am leaving no less than three almost perfectly happy couples!" (314).

A contemporary reviewer found that the six heroes and heroines made the plot confusing.[4] But *Bird of Paradise* is like *Tenterhooks* in having a coherent (though much more elaborate) narrative line, the impetus of which is seldom frittered away in digressions. It is also like *Tenterhooks* in its increased attention to the exploration of psychological states and in its more forthright recognition of sexuality. Like all the other novels, *Bird of Paradise* concerns love, courtship, romance, marriage, and jealousy.

## II *Word-of-All-Work*

C. P. Snow said of Mrs. Leverson that she wrote wisely and honestly about the emotions of love,[5] and *Bird of Paradise* especially justifies his opinion. The note of questing and probing in the passages which most directly concern the mysterious subject of love marks the depth of Mrs. Leverson's inquiries; for love in itself is so often inconclusive that conclusions about it must be tentative. Nigel's thoughts about Bertha are an example: "And his love for Bertha—what word can one use but the word-of-all-work, love, which means so many variations and shades, and complications of passion, sentiment, vanity and attraction?—his love had greatly increased, was growing stronger: sometimes he wondered whether it was the mere contradictory, defiant obstinacy of the discouraged admirer; and, certainly, there was in his devotion a strong infusion of a longing to score off his tyrannising wife and the fortunate, amiable Percy" (78).

From Charlie Hillier's honest young love to his brother Nigel's complex attitude, from Madeline's pupil-like worship of Rupert to Bertha's adult passion for her husband, Mrs. Leverson is a wise explorer. Many incidental and brief passages are particularly thoughtful, as when she divides men as lovers into hunters and collectors (78, 101). The hunter category is clear and familiar, the frustrations of the chase adding to its excitement; the collector is he who regards his wife as a valuable object, and Percy Kellynch is something of one, just as Lord Chetwode in *The Twelfth Hour* and Lord Selsey in *Love's Shadow* pronouncedly are.

In Mrs. Leverson's thinking, love is inseparable from jealousy, as a synopsis of the plot of any of her novels reveals. And *Bird of*

*Paradise* is her fullest statement on jealousy—it dominates intermittently or consistently Rupert, Madeline, Nigel, Percy—in fact, everyone but Bertha; and most of all it makes Mary Hillier its victim. She is a superb study. Even her ordinary manner suggests the emotion: "There was something eager, sharp and yet depressed about her, that might well be irritating" (65). Jealousy does not merely dominate her life; it has become her life: "She suspected him of infidelity, with and without reason, morning, noon, and night; it was almost a monomania" (42). Each day she sits in agitated vigil, watching by the window for Nigel's return; she questions him with undisguised avidity about his activities, or she tries to wheedle her way into his favor by playing maddeningly with his tie or talking babytalk. At its most savage, her jealousy goads her into tantrums, screams, breaking vases. The obsessions of jealousy can make its victims abandon society, and this has happened to Mary. She no longer receives or goes out, for, as she says of the parties they gave in the early years of their marriage, "I hated them and loathed them. . . . For it only meant there were crowds of women who tried to flirt with you" (67). What Bertha's good advice to Mary amounts to is to dissipate somehow the fury of jealous love, to disguise it by ordinary cheerfulness, to love and cherish her children so that Nigel will be grateful to her for being a good mother. Bertha's advice may be a little pat, and Mary's reform a little facile. Or it may only be that a reader is reluctant to part with those theatrical intensities in which Mary, when most the prey of the monster, moves.

Bertha, with her clearsightedness, and also with a touch of naïveté, rejoices in jealousy as the one sure sign:

> Her eyes sparkled. She stood up beaming radiant joy. She went to him impulsively; everything was all right; he was jealous! (146)
>
> . . .
>
> "Oh, Percy, *how* sweet of you to say that! You're becoming a regular jealous husband, do you know? Darling! How delightful!" (191)

Bertha's enthusiasm may be appealing, but Mary's jealousy is hideous. That the one sure sign of love, which is itself a creative force, can cause such destruction as the twisted personality of Mary Hillier is an anomaly which Mrs. Leverson analyzes, and with no easy conclusions, in *Bird of Paradise.*

## III *Happy Eclecticism*

Despite the serious tone of many sections, *Bird of Paradise* is a return to a lighter mood than *Tenterhooks.* Her most joyous book, *The Twelfth Hour,* is the least organized of the six; but her fifth novel, while embodying much of pure plot interest, has its excursions into comedy, and the humorous characters in it are more openly funny than corresponding figures in *Tenterhooks.* Mrs. Pickering, formerly a principal boy in a pantomime but now the wife of a millionaire on Park Lane, with her too-golden hair and her violet satin boots with fur round the edge (217), could have been a snob's view of an *arriviste* if Thackeray or Evelyn Waugh had created her, but in Mrs. Leverson's hands she is harmless and rather appealing. Mrs. Leverson was never a snob about her characters, but she was acutely aware of the shades of class distinction. Mrs. Pickering is idolized by the fourteen-year-old Clifford Kellynch, who, like the sixteen-year-old Savile Crofton in *The Twelfth Hour,* dislikes cant, upholds the proprieties, and is both romantic and conservative, though he is not old enough to have attained Savile's aplomb and managerial efficiency. Incidental figures in *Bird of Paradise* like Bevan Fairfield, a dandy, have also been seen in other guises before, as well as the fancy dress balls he likes to attend: "The last one I went to I had a great success as a forget-me-not" (260). At this ball, he had met an elephant which contained the Mitchells, that party-loving couple who appear in the Ottley novels.

Mrs. Leverson makes us see these minor figures with something of her own clarity and sense of the ridiculous. We particularly share the keenness of observation in her description of the dress of the esthetic Miss Belvoir, where, like Keats with the Grecian urn, we almost become part of the life of the object viewed:

> Indeed her costume was so uncommon as to be on the verge of eccentricity. Her face had a slightly Japanese look, and she increased this effect by wearing a gown of which a part was decidedly Japanese. In fact it was a kimono covered with embroidery in designs consisting of a flight of storks, some chrysanthemums, and a few butterflies, in the richest shades of blue. In the lefthand corner were two little yellow men fighting with a sword in each hand; otherwise it was all blue. It was almost impossible to keep one's eyes from this yellow duel; the little embroidered figures looked so fierce and emotional and appeared to be enjoying themselves so much. (256–57)

Lady Gertrude Münster appears for a few pages, and Mrs. Leverson evokes her with such deftness and ease that one wishes she were more than a figure briefly met at a tea party: "She was a clever, glib, battered-looking, elderly woman, who, since her husband had once been at the Embassy in Vienna, had assumed a slight foreign accent; it was meant to be Austrian but sounded Scotch. Lady Gertrude looked rather muffled and seemed to have more thick veils and feather boas on than was necessary for the time of the year. She was an old friend of Lady Kellynch's, and they detested each other . . ." (220).

Lady Münster's enemy in the Dowager Wars, Lady Kellynch, is the mother of Percy and Clifford Kellynch and is, with Lady Cannon in *Love's Shadow*, the stupidest of Mrs. Leverson's dowagers. She is based on two figures, the first and second wives of George Leverson, Ernest Leverson's father.[6] One supposes that, had Mrs. Leverson written twenty novels instead of six, there would be in them twenty distinctly conceived dowagers, so expert was she in ringing the changes on the type: "Lady Kellynch never got away from 1887 and the time of Queen Victoria's first Jubilee. All the fads of the hour seemed to have passed over her since then, from bicycling to flying, from classical dancing or ragtime to enthusiasm about votes for women; the various movements had passed over her without leaving any hurt or effect. Lady Kellynch had had a success in 1887 . . ." (211).

But Lady Kellynch is like Lady Cannon and others in remaining, like a fly in amber, fixated in her heyday. Her uniqueness lies in the stateliness of her stupidity: "She was at once vague and precise, quite amiable, very sentimental and utterly heartless; except to her sons" (28). In the following passage she is reading "purple patches" from Clifford's school report: " '*Music and dancing: music, rather weak . . . dancing, a steady worker.*' That's very good, isn't it? . . . '*Map-drawing: very slovenly.*' " (She read this rather proudly.) " '*Conduct: lethargic and unsteady; but a fair speller.*' Excellent, isn't it?" (31).

Mrs. Leverson was by now over fifty, but the delighted shrewdness of her pictures of Lady Kellynch, Lady Gertrude Münster, and the rest show how very far she was from becoming a dowager herself. The comedy of *Bird of Paradise*, despite its echoes and the intensities of love and jealousy it dramatizes, is as youthful in spirit as ever.

## CHAPTER 10

# Love at Second Sight

### I *World War I*

"THE dinner was bright and gay from the very beginning, even before the first glass of champagne. It began with an optimistic view of the war, then, dropping the grave subject, they talked of people, theatres, books, and general gossip" (51). The dinner is given by Bruce and Edith Ottley in honor of their house guest, Madame Eglantine Frabelle, who is the English widow of a French wine merchant. "People, theatre, books, and general gossip" are what Mrs. Leverson's people usually talk about in the six novels; they avoid "grave subjects" like God and religion, war and crime, good and evil. To reviewers of the 1950 and 1951 reprints of Mrs. Leverson's novels—who approached them only as "soufflés" and as mementoes of the "sunny" era of the Edwardians and who had vivid memories of an even more hideous war—it often seemed appropriate that her writing career ended with World War I and with the Edwardian era which that war in fact, if not quite chronologically, ended. Yet Mrs. Leverson, if not always her characters in their conversation, could and did deal with "grave subjects"; and, rather than dismissing the war, she in fact constructed her sixth and last novel around it. The war dictates the structure and the meaning of *Love at Second Sight*, which was published in the middle of World War I in 1916.

She does not treat the subject gingerly; nor does she allow the impression that she acknowledges it dutifully or intermittently only before returning to congenial frivolity. The war is so woven into the ideological tissue of *Love at Second Sight*, that it becomes part of Mrs. Leverson's habitual apparatus of satire. The women in the novel have studied nursing or do volunteer work for the refugees, and Madame Frabelle is especially active in these efforts. Rich and comfortable parasite in the Ottley household,

Madame Frabelle at another dinner party "lectured on 'dress and economy in war-time,' and how to manage a house on next to nothing a year" (175–76).

Madame Frabelle's rival in fatuity, Bruce Ottley, who has been kept out of military service by a "neurotic heart" (229), exchanges at the same party symptoms with a group of "war valetudinarians"; and, after visiting his friend Aylmer Ross, who is convalescing from wounds received at the front, he returns home and enters his wife's drawing room "holding himself very straight with a slightly military manner. When he saw his wife, he just stopped himself from saluting" (126). As selfish and egotistic as he was in *Love's Shadow* or *Tenterhooks*—Bruce learns nothing through the years—his farewell to Edith as she leaves for a brief stay at the seaside is typical: " 'Perhaps we shall never meet again,' said Bruce pleasantly, as Edith, Dilly and the nurse were starting; 'either the Zeppelins may come while you're away, or they may set your hotel at Eastcliff on fire. Just the place for them' " (287).

The war-focused satire extends to minor characters like the stepmother of Aylmer Ross's beautiful young nurse, Dulcie Clay. Mrs. Clay, though her husband is virtually bankrupt through his losses at the track, begs money from Dulcie, declaring that one is "expected to dress up to a certain standard, though, of course, simply during war-time" (187). A far more amiable character is Lady Conroy, an absent-minded Irishwoman who is so forgetful that her friends allege she cannot remember the names of her seven children. We have a typical glimpse of her: "Let me pour it out,' said Edith, to whom it was maddening to see the curious things Lady Conroy did with the tea-tray. She was pouring tea into the sugar basin, looking up at Edith with the sweetest smile" (p. 214). But even Lady Conroy's mind can be brought into dizzy focus on the war: as she says to Dulcie Clay, who becomes her companion when Aylmer Ross no longer needs Dulcie as his nurse, "We'll go to some of those all-British concerts, won't we? We must be patriotic" (243).

Thus, whether it is Madame Frabelle's wartime economies or Bruce's neurotic heart or Lady Conroy's all-British concerts, attitudes toward the war are subjects for Mrs. Leverson's alert comedy. But in the love story itself the war is central. In *Tenterhooks* Aylmer Ross had left Edith Ottley because, though she had legal reason for divorce in her husband's infidelity, she would not use it. Now, three years later, Aylmer returns, even more attractive to her as a wounded war hero. Edith has a "slight contempt" for Bruce and his imaginary heart ailment; and, when Aylmer agains requests her to leave Bruce—a request now rendered far more urgent because Aylmer, when restored to health, will return to the front—she hesitates.

She discusses her hesitation only with Sir Tito Landi, a friend since girlhood, who now occupies the role of confidant which was held by Hyacinth Verney in *Love's Shadow* and by Vincy in *Tenterhooks.* The original of Landi, according to Violet Wyndham, was Paolo Tosti, author of the famous "Good-bye" and many other songs. A friend for many years of Mrs. Leverson, he dedicated one or two of his songs to Violet, Ada's youngest sister.[1] Some critics have enjoyed the Latin aplomb and suavity of Landi, but his advice to Edith can become tedious, as can his flirtatiousness, his heavy paternalism, his rich old Italian wisdom. He is a well-realized character that the reader likes less than his creator did.

Nonetheless, he can explain to Edith as she cannot to herself why she now hesitates, where before she was unshaken in her decision to let Aylmer go. Of the war, Landi says, "Unconsciously it affects people. Though you yourself are not fighting Aylmer has risked his life, and is going to risk it again. This impresses you. To many temperaments things seem to matter less just now. People are reckless" (220). Since convention, as much as anything else, had caused Edith to remain with Bruce in the past, she realizes the truth of what Landi tells her: though she has detested the idea of publicity and vulgar scandal, she admits that they do not "seem to matter now so much" (211); and, if tacitly, she confesses the truth of Aylmer's question: "But don't you see, Edith, that if you still like me, your present life is a long slow sacrifice to convention, or (as you say) to a morbid sense of responsibility?" (155).

The war destroyed conventions of the sort which had governed Edith's earlier decision. She now decides to accept Aylmer—to agree to divorce Bruce when Aylmer, the war over, can return to her permanently. Thinking of Aylmer's own heroism, she has begged Landi to encourage her to break with convention: "Don't let me be a coward! Think if Aylmer goes out again and is killed, how miserable I should feel to have refused him and disappointed him—for the second time!" (222).

The moral growth of Edith from *Tenterhooks* to *Love at Second Sight* is clearly revealed in her decision. An independent and thoughtful courage replaces her conventional courage of the past. And it is beautifully right that her decision should be made before the group of events which obviates it: Bruce, who has eloped before, elopes with Madame Frabelle to America; and Aylmer, instead of returning to the front, is given an assignment in the War Office in London. However, the war is inseparable from Bruce's own motives in leaving Edith. He may momentarily admire Aylmer, the war hero, and momentarily affect rather pathetic military stances of his own; but his hypochondria becomes violent because of the war, and his decision to leave Edith is a decision to leave the war. From the beginning, he has mysteriously associated Madame Frabelle with possibilities of escape. "His neurotic heart bored his friends at the club" (269); but Madame Frabelle takes his ailments seriously. He early becomes the invalid he has long fancied himself to be because of the war he "hated": "Edith was convinced that he was positively jealous of the general interest in it!" (269).

When, at the end of the novel, Bruce tells Edith that he is leaving her, his reason is not, as it was in the case of Mavis Argles three years earlier, "Madame Frabelle and I are all in all to each other" (for after all, Eglantine, however fascinating to him, is fifteen years older than he), but an overruling cowardice with genuinely physical symptoms: "I find I can no longer endure to live in London; I must get away from the war" (300). The war brings out the worst in Bruce, just as it brings out the best in Edith; to her, the effect is a farewell to cant, a more intelligent idea of moral responsibility, and a courage that strives to emulate the heroism of her lover.

## II *The Marriage of True Minds*

In considering Mrs. Leverson's novels in order, one is struck by the following series of facts: In *The Twelfth Hour*, Felicity and Chetwode have been married one year; in *Love's Shadow*, Edith and Bruce have been married three years; in *The Limit*, Valentia and Romer have been married five years; in *Tenterhooks*, Edith and Bruce have been married eight years; in *Bird of Paradise*, Bertha and Percy have been married ten years; and in *Love at Second Sight*, Edith and Bruce have been married eleven, or possibly twelve, years. It is unlikely that this time scheme is planned, but it is certainly related to the autobiographical elements in the novels. Indeed, both internal evidence and external fact indicate that Mrs. Leverson's own marriage contributed to making this situation her basic theme.

It is easy to see that Edith and Aylmer will be a happily married couple since they both have that quality of absoluteness which hero and heroine inherit as a birthright. We may not be stirred by their marriage, but we know that it is proper and fitting. Edith was twenty-eight in *Tenterhooks;* only three years have elapsed; but now, in *Love at Second Sight,* she is thirty-five (145). Aylmer was forty in the earlier novel; three years later, he is not forty-three, but forty-two (106), and once he calls himself forty-one (158). These discrepancies are caused by that idealizing urge we have spoken of before in relation to Mrs. Leverson's heroes and heroines. The union between Edith and Aylmer must be perfectly matched in age, temperament, and tastes; Aylmer is already rich, and Edith has her own income (Bruce has his and Eglantine's); even the children must be demonstrably happy at the loss of their father in exchange for a better one. For example, when, little Dilly's toy balloon bursts, to her sorrow, Aylmer runs after the balloon-seller (though the noble fellow still limps) to buy her two more (294–95), and Archie says unkindly of the weakling Bruce ,"I wish I had a father who could fight, like Aylmer" (239).

The sexual attraction between Aylmer and Edith is more powerfully expressed by his refusal to kiss her—"I can't kiss people" (266; he means that he cannot *just* kiss people)—than by the pages of explicit detail a contemporary novel would devote to it. Edith is a more attractive woman than she was in *Tenterhooks;* her conflicts are dramatized, not resolved by easy recourse to moral conventions. The degree of her triumph is intensified even by such minor matters as her lack of jealousy of Aylmer's beautiful young nurse Dulcie, who is much in love with him. Mrs. Leverson has finally written a novel in which jealousy is not essential to the story; the loss is credibility, and the gain is allegory.

It is not quite so obvious a matter that Bruce Ottley and Eglantine Frabelle are another ideal pair. For one reason, we are used to Bruce; for another, Eglantine is Mrs. Leverson's greatest single character, and her personality is too engrossingly unique for the question of a suitable mate for her to seem a relevant one. But Bruce is her match, and the step-by-step process from acquaintance to flirtation to infatuation to elopement, which is presented with the most skillful articulation, helps to dramatize him. As is usual, the person most concerned is the least aware: Edith finds Madame Frabelle too fascinating, is herself too absorbed in the reawakening of love for Aylmer, and is too bored with Bruce to see what others see.

Early in the novel Landi says of Frabelle, "Elle est folle de ton mari!" (55). A little later, the elder Mrs. Ottley slyly questions Edith, "And she keeps Bruce in a good temper?" (67). Madame Frabelle herself remarks laughingly to Edith, "I even feel sometimes . . . as if it would be a pleasure to look after him, take care of him. I think it would not have been a bad thing for him to have married a woman a little older than himself. But you, Edith, you're so young" (86). And Aylmer comments to Edith, "Probably already he's in love with that woman What's-her-name—Madame Frabelle—who's staying with you" (152). Edith is either deaf to these comments, or doesn't care.

The dawn and the development of this grotesque romance, or this romance between grotesques, are sketched in scene after scene:

> "Lady Conroy," said Bruce thoughtfully, at breakfast next day, "is a very strict Roman Catholic."
>
> Bruce was addicted to volunteering information, and making unanswerable remarks.
>
> Madame Frabelle said to Edith in a low, earnest tone:
>
> "Pass me the butter, dear," and looked attentively at Bruce. (109)

Chapter VII, devoted to Bruce and Madame Frabelle's expedition on the river, is surely the drollest chapter Mrs. Leverson ever wrote, with its mixture of boredom, flirtation, frustration, irritation—for, in fact, the relationship is not so much love as the irresistible joining of two complementary monoliths. "Bruce was more genuinely impressed and unconsciously bored by Madame Frabelle than by any woman he had ever met," Mrs. Leverson tells us at the outset (14). Frabelle's interest in other men, such as the Reverend Byrne Fraser (a society clergyman, "a handsome weary-looking man of whom more was supposed than could conveniently be said" [88]), is genuine; but he is also used to spur Bruce on.

Frabelle's principal artillery, however, is a power of hypnosis—the word is used of her several times (16, 52)—which has a perverse humor of its own, because, though she can somehow enter among the mental processes of another person, she invariably misinterprets them. It is often said that Frabelle has the gift of second sight—"Elle voit double"—but her perceptions are always distorted. In the following passage, the end results justify her original misconception:

> She was beginning to fear that Bruce was getting too fond of her.
> The moment the idea occurred to her, it occurred to Bruce also. She had a hypnotic effect on him; as soon as she thought of anything he thought of it too. Something in her slight change of manner, her cautious way of answering, and of rustling self-consciously out of the room when they were left alone together, had this effect. Bruce was enchanted. Madame Frabelle thought he was getting too fond of her! Then, he must be! Perhaps he was. (228–29)

Eglantine is created with endless richness of detail:

> She was inclined to be fat; not locally, in the manner of a pincushion, but with the generally diffused plumpness described in shops as stock size. (15)
>
> . . .
>
> Madame Frabelle (of course) was dressed in black, *décolletée,* and with a good deal of jet. A black aigrette, like a lightning conductor, stood up defiantly in her hair . . . Madame Frabelle really would have looked her best in a cap of the fashion of the sixties. But she could carry off anything; and some people said that she did. (46–47)
>
> . . .
>
> . . . All her notions of life were taken from the stage. She looked upon existence from the theatrical point of view. Everyone was to her a hero or heroine, a villain or a victim. To her a death was a *dénouement;* a marriage a happy ending. (101)

Mrs. Leverson sums up her character's hypnotic fascination in a single sentence: "People were not charmed with Eglantine because she herself was charming, but because she was charmed" (53). Grand fake that she is, she belongs with Bruce, the monster of egotism who has finally found someone sympathetic to the point of idiocy. Both Edith and Aylmer have a strong penchant for comedy; neither Bruce nor Madame Frabelle has an ounce: "It flashed across Edith what an immense bond of sympathy it was between Bruce and Madame Frabelle that neither of them was burdened with the slightest sense of humour" (33). The aptest stroke of all is that this lack is exactly the fault Madame Frabelle finds with Aylmer:

> "The fact is, he has no sense of humour," said Madame Frabelle.
> "Fancy your finding that out now!" said Bruce, with a broad smile. "Funny! Ha ha! Very funny!" (260)

V. S. Pritchett has written of her: "She is the Life Force gone dowdy, shady and kind, but never dormant. Indeed, advancing years make her phoneyness redoubtable. It is she who runs off with Bruce in the end—one can imagine her picking him up like a puppy in her teeth and wobbling off with him. . . . When she carries off Bruce, no one really minds. Two absurdities will have fulfilled themselves. Edith's excellences bored Bruce: he needed the dramatic companionship of a fellow self-deceiver."[2] We expect the hero and heroine to live happily ever after; but one of the joys of *Love at Second Sight* is that the splendid duo of fools has an equally roseate future.

## III *Transitions*

Robert Ross, Mrs. Leverson's friend to whom both *The Limit* and *Tenterhooks* were dedicated, wrote to her after reading *Love at Second Sight:* "I have been able to delight in *Love at Second Sight*. . . . I don't think, however, I can ever forgive you for throwing away Frabelle—you must write another book about her and mention how she missed the boat at Liverpool and wasn't allowed to sail with Bruce. She is a really great impressionist picture by Whistler or Manet. . . ."[3] But Mrs. Leverson published no more novels: which somehow seems to make significant the dedication of this last novel—to "Tacitus," her name for Grant Richards, who had encouraged her to begin writing novels many years earlier and whose firm published her six books.

## IV *Conclusion*

The articulation of plot, the by now quite un-Victorian treatment of sexuality, the increasing authority of psychological analysis, the sureness of comic powers which could embrace even a war and make it part of the novel's structure—these excellences and others support the opinion of a reviewer in 1951 who said that Mrs. Leverson's later novels "illustrate the transition from the Victorian domestic to the emancipated modern novel."[4] Colin MacInnes has pointed out that "even the decorative chapter headings of the earlier five books have vanished in the assured pace with which she sets down her final testament."[5] Inez Holden wrote, "There were very few writers with her ear for dialogue then, and very few who can equal her dialogue now."[6]

Mrs. Leverson was at the top of her powers. If her novels should, in terms of literary history, be called transitional works, such a designation only places, not judges, them. Her novel-writing career came to a close like her chapters, which often end with such brilliant suddenness. But though there are only the six short books, they present a complete world, densely populated and lavishly described, and a singularly shrewd but delighted comic vision of human beings. The one way in which her novels most aptly can be called transitional is that they are the last example of a serious, bright, and hopeful comedy that we have, before the solemn dark comedies of the present day began.

# *Notes and References*

## *Chapter One*

1. Violet Wyndham, *The Sphinx and Her Circle: A Memoir of Ada Leverson by Her Daughter* (London: André Deutsch, 1963; New York: Vanguard, 1964).
2. *Ibid.*, New York edition, pp. 13–15.
3. *Ibid.*, p. 15.
4. *Ibid.*, pp. 16–17, 19, 39, 77.
5. *Ibid.*, p. 94.
6. *Ibid.*, pp. 21–23, 29–31, 89–90.
7. *Ibid.*, p. 24. Sir Osbert Sitwell places the meeting of Mrs. Leverson and Wilde a year later, in 1893, after her parody of *Dorian Gray* had appeared in *Punch* (July 15, 1893); see *Noble Essences* (Boston: Little, Brown, 1950), pp. 154–55.
8. *Ibid.*, p. 154.
9. Rupert Hart-Davis, ed., *The Letters of Oscar Wilde* (New York: Harcourt, Brace & World, 1962), pp. 344, 373.
10. *Ibid.*, p. 357, n. 4.
11. *Ibid.*, pp. 372–73.
12. *Ibid.*, p. 357, n. 3.
13. *Letters to the Sphinx from Oscar Wilde, with Reminiscences of the Author* (London: Duckworth; printed in 275 signed copies).
14. Hart-Davis, p. x.
15. Part of the essay appeared under the title "The Last First Night" in *Criterion*, IV (January, 1926), 148–53.
16. Hart-Davis, pp. 527, 539, 540, 541, 550, 552.
17. Her contributions to *Punch* and other periodicals are discussed in Chapter 3.
18. Grant Richards, *Memories of a Misspent Youth* (London: William Heinemann, 1932), p. 300.
19. *Ibid.*
20. Wyndham, p. 63.
21. Sir William Rothenstein, *Since Fifty: Men and Memories, 1922–1938* (New York: Macmillan, 1940), p. 139.

22. Stanley Weintraub, *Reggie: A Portrait of Reginald Turner* (New York: G. Braziller, 1965), pp. 139–40.

23. Harold Acton, *Memoirs of an Aesthete* (London: Methuen, 1948), p. 381.

24. Sitwell, p. 154.

25. *Ibid.*, pp. 152–53.

26. *Ibid.*, p. 170.

27. *Ibid.*, p. 151.

28. *Ibid.*, pp. 165–66.

29. *Ibid.*, pp. 147–48.

30. Joseph Hone, *The Life of George Moore* (London: Victor Gollancz, 1936), p. 459.

31. So many motives and symbolisms and attitudes enter into Wyndham Lewis' caricature of Mrs. Leverson (whom he calls the "Sib") in *Apes of God* (London: Arthur Press, 1930) that its usefulness as a portrait is nearly nil. See especially pp. 353–79 *passim*, 495–98, 552, 582.

32. Wyndham, p. 20.

33. Weedon and George Grossmith's *The Diary of a Nobody* was first published in 1892; an available edition is that of Alfred Knopf (New York, 1923); it contains illustrations by Weedon Grossmith and a memoir of the brothers by B. W. Findon.

34. "Anthony Hope's" *The Dolly Dialogues* was first published in 1894; the best edition—because it has illustrations perfectly in period by Howard Chandler Christy—was published in New York by R. H. Russell in 1901.

35. *The Bodley Head Saki*, ed. J. W. Lambert (London: The Bodley Head, 1963), p. 77.

36. *Ibid.*, p. 371.

## *Chapter Two*

1. Some would add theme, and perhaps one or two others. But theme is a function of plot, character, and setting, rather than itself an ingredient in the recipe for fiction. Moreover, a theme does not always exist.

2. José Ortega y Gasset, *The Dehumanization of Art and Notes on the Novel*, trans. Helene Weyl (Princeton: Princeton University Press, 1948), p. 90.

3. In Henry James's famous essay of 1884, "The Art of Fiction." Often reprinted, a convenient edition is *The Portable Henry James*, ed. Morton Dauwen Zabel (New York: Viking, 1951), p. 403.

4. *Referee*, May 28, 1905, p. 9.

5. Page references are to the reissue of the six novels by Chapman and Hall in 1950–51. First editions of the novels are by now far too rare to be conveniently cited.

6. Wyndham, p. 29.
7. *Ibid.*, p. 28. Paquin still exists at 50 Grosvenor Street, W.1.
8. *Ibid.*, pp. 65, 73, 82.
9. *Ibid.*, p. 39.
10. *The Little Ottleys* brought together in one volume *Love's Shadow, Tenterhooks,* and *Love at Second Sight.* It was published in London by MacGibbon and Kee in 1962 and in New York by Norton in 1963. In the latter edition, Mr. MacInnes' comments on Mrs. Leverson and art are in his introduction, p. 14, footnote.

## *Chapter Three*

1. *Letters to the Sphinx from Oscar Wilde* (London: Duckworth, 1930), p. 52. Rupert Hart-Davis, in his edition of *The Letters of Oscar Wilde* (New York: Harcourt, Brace & World, 1962, p. 343), uses Mrs. Leverson's text of the letter and dates it "[? Circa 15 July 1893]".
2. Wyndham, p. 64.
3. And what I know I owe almost entirely to the help of Violet Wyndham and the great generosity with which she made family papers available.
4. Wyndham, p. 26.
5. *Ibid.*, p. 43.
6. Respectively: *Black and White,* IV (October 15, 1892), 447–51; IV (December 10, 1892), 678–80; VII (January 6, 1894), 18–22.
7. *Black and White,* VI (August 5, 1893), 160, was Letter #1; *Black and White,* VII (January 27, 1894), 117–20, was Letter #24. For a complete list, see the bibliography of Mrs. Leverson's writings.
8. Wyndham, p. 19: "Marguerite Leverson, Ernest's first cousin, married Brandon Thomas, the author of *Charley's Aunt.* The play was almost a family affair, as the name 'Charley' was taken from that of Ada's brother."
9. For exact dates of the letters and stories see bibliography of Mrs. Leverson's writings.
10. Wyndham, pp. 26–27.
11. A complete listing is given in the bibliography of Mrs. Leverson's writings.
12. Once again, it is likely that there are more short pieces of this nature, but they have not as yet been found.
13. *Punch,* CIV (July 15, 1893), 13.
14. See footnote 8, above.
15. *Punch,* CVII (July 21, 1894), 33.
16. *Letters to the Sphinx,* p. 50.
17. *Punch,* CVIII (January 13, 1895), 24.
18. *Ibid.* (March 2, 1895), 107.
19. Wyndham, p. 38.

20. *Punch,* CVIII (October 27, 1894), 204.

21. *Sketch,* VIII (January 2, 1895), 439; published in its entirety in Wyndham, pp. 45–48.

22. *Punch,* CVIII (February 2, 1895), 58, and CIX (December 21, 1895), 297.

23. *Ibid.,* CIX (September 21, 1895), 141.

24. *Ibid.,* CIX (November 30, 1895), 264.

25. *Ibid.,* CXIII (July 17, 1897), 16–17.

26. The portrait appears in *Yellow Book,* V (April, 1895), 231. Mrs. Wyndham calls it "extremely unflattering" (Wyndham, 44); Osbert Sitwell calls it "a delightful portrait drawing," p. 161.

27. Respectively: *Yellow Book,* V (April, 1895), 249–57; and VIII (January, 1896), 325–35.

## *Chapter Four*

1. In letters to Alec Ross, Robert Ross's brother, in the possession of Robert Ross's great-nephew, Mr. J.-P. R. Ross, Mrs. Leverson says that the name of her book on Robert Ross was to be "A Modern Memory: Recollections of Robert Ross and Some of His Friends." On October 18, 1918, she says, "I have put aside my novel for the present."

2. Wyndham, pp. 40–42.

3. There was no column in the issue of June 5, 1904.

4. Other reasons why Mrs. Leverson began to write novels are suggested in Chapter 1.

5. "Free Verse," *English Review,* XXIX (December, 1919), 534–36.

6. "The Blow," *English Review,* XXXI (December, 1920), 515–20. Also published in *Living Age,* CCCVIII (January 8, 1921), 111–14.

7. *Letters to the Sphinx from Oscar Wilde,* p. 51.

8. "Gentlemen v. Players," *English Review,* XXXIV (April, 1922), 331–34.

9. *Letters to the Sphinx from Oscar Wilde,* pp. 19–20. Mrs. Leverson had been amused by the amount of margin in *Silverpoints* (1893), the first book of her friend the young poet John Gray. See Stanley Weintraub, *Beardsley* (New York: Braziller, 1967), pp. 73–74.

10. *Criterion,* IV (January, 1926), 148–53.

11. Quoted in Wyndham, p. 98.

12. Mrs. Leverson's footnote explains that this lady "was the beautiful Mrs. Carew, the mother of Sir Coleridge Kennard."

## *Chapter Five*

1. Colin MacInnes, "The Heart of a Legend," *Encounter,* XVI (May, 1961), 51.

2. G. W. Stonier, review of *Love's Shadow* and *The Limit*; and of

*The Twelfth Hour* and *Bird of Paradise, New Statesman,* n.s. XLIII (January 5, 1952), 16.

3. William Cox, "Back to Golden Afternoon," review of *Tenterhooks* and *Love at Second Sight, Yorkshire Observer,* August 2, 1951, p. 7.

4. "The Edwardians," review of *Love's Shadow* and *The Limit, Sunday Times,* November 12, 1950, p. 3.

5. Wyndham, p. 17.

6. *Ibid.*, p. 82.

7. Review of *The Twelfth Hour, Bookman,* XXXII (August, 1907), 108.

8. *Review of The Twelfth Hour, Westminster Gazette,* XXIX (April 15, 1907), 3.

9. Review of *The Twelfth Hour, Academy,* LXXII (April 6, 1907), 344.

*Chapter Six*

1. "Visiting the Sphinx," review of *The Limit* and *Love's Shadow, Times Literary Supplement,* December 29, 1950, p. 825.

2. Review of *Love's Shadow, Academy,* LXXIV (June 20, 1908), 909.

3. "The Wittiest Woman in the World," review of *The Limit* and *Love's Shadow, Britain Today,* April, 1951, n.p.

4. "The Knightsbridge Kennels," review of *The Little Ottleys, New Statesman,* LXIV (August 31, 1962), 257.

*Chapter Seven*

1. Review of *The Limit, Daily Telegraph,* March 1, 1911, p. 14.

2. Review of *The Limit, Star,* March 18, 1911, p. 2.

3. Review of *The Limit, Vanity Fair,* LXXXVI (March 15, 1911), 298.

4. Review of *The Limit, Referee,* March 5, 1911, p. 6.

5. Review of *The Limit, Graphic,* LXXXIII (April 1, 1911), 478.

6. Review of *The Limit, Pelican,* XLVI (March 15, 1911), 11.

7. Review of *The Limit, Morning Post,* March 30, 1911, p. 2.

8. Review of *The Limit, World,* LXXIV (April 4, 1911), 500.

9. Review of *The Limit, Westminster Gazette,* XXXVII (April 1, 1911), 7.

10. Review of *The Limit, Morning Leader,* March 29, 1911, p. 2.

11. Review of *The Limit, Standard,* March 17, 1911, p. 5.

12. Leo Lerman "Select and Edwardian," review of *The Limit, New York Times,* August 19, 1951, p. 4.

13. Inez Holden, "The Art of Ada Leverson," *Cornhill Magazine,* CLXIV (Summer, 1950), 433.

14. "Visiting the Sphinx," review of *Love's Shadow* and *The Limit, Times Literary Supplement,* December 29, 1950, p. 825.

15. Adrian Alington, review of *Love's Shadow* and *The Limit, Public Opinion,* December 8, 1950, p. 18.

16. Colin MacInnes, "The Heart of a Legend," *Encounter*, XVI (May, 1961), 51.

17. The original of this character was Cosmo Gordon-Lennox, Wyndham, p. 74: "He bubbled over with gaiety, charm and good nature, wrote plays and sometimes appeared on the stage himself. . . . He married the actress Marie Tempest with disastrous results to him. Whatever his faults may have been, and his wife discovered that these included at least one of Oscar Wilde's, he was a man it was impossible not to like when in his company. He had the gift of making life fun. He did not lack kindness nor courage either, and won admiration for both during the First World War. He died soon after the Armistice."

18. *Letters to the Sphinx from Oscar Wilde*, pp. 63, 45.

19. Wyndham, p. 72.

## *Chapter Eight*

1. Max Beerbohm, *Letters to Reggie Turner*, ed. Rupert Hart-Davis (London: Rupert Hart-Davis, 1964), p. 216.

2. L. A. G. Strong, "Edwardian Summers," review of *Tenterhooks* and *Love at Second Sight, Public Opinion*, June 15, 1951, p. 21.

3. "The Edwardians," review of *Tenterhooks* and *Love at Second Sight, Times Literary Supplement*, March 23, 1951, p. 177.

4. "The Sphinx's Soufflés," review of *The Little Ottleys, Times*, August 23, 1962, p. 11.

5. "The Heart of a Legend," *Encounter*, XVI (May, 1961), 54.

## *Chapter Nine*

1. "Letters of Marjorie and Gladys," *Punch*, CXI (December 12, 1896), 277.

2. *Letters to the Sphinx from Oscar Wilde*, p. 63.

3. *Ibid.*, p. 51.

4. Review of *Bird of Paradise, Bookman*, XLVI (September, 1914), 253.

5. Review of *Love's Shadow* and *The Limit, Spectator*, CLXXVI (January 19, 1951), 82.

6. Wyndham, pp. 17–18.

## *Chapter Ten*

1. Wyndham, p. 33.

2. "The Knightsbridge Kennels," review of *The Little Ottleys, New Statesman*, LXIV (August 31, 1962), 257.

3. Wyndham, p. 78.

4. Conrad Howe, "Leverson on Love," review of *Tenterhooks* and *Love at Second Sight*, *Liverpool Daily Post*, April 3, 1951, p. 3.

5. Colin MacInnes, "The Heart of a Legend," *Encounter*, XVI (May, 1961), 55.

6. Inez Holden, "The Art of Ada Leverson," *Cornhill Magazine*, CLXIV (Summer, 1950), 431.

# *Selected Bibliography*


PRIMARY SOURCES

(This listing of Leverson's works is chronologically arranged.)

"Claude's Aunt," *Black and White*, IV (October 15, 1892), 447–51.

"Mimosa," *Black and White*, IV (December 10, 1892), 678–80.

"An Afternoon Party," *Punch*, CIV (July 15, 1893), 13.

"Letters of Silvia and Aurelia, I–XXIV," *Black and White*, VI and VII (August 5, 1893, to January 27, 1894). I: VI (August 5, 1893), 160. II: VI (August 12, 1893), 192. III: VI (August 19, 1893), 218–19. IV: VI (August 26, 1893), 252. V: VI (September 2, 1893), 301. VI: VI (September 9, 1893), 314. VII: VI (September 16, 1893), 345–46. VIII: VI (September 23, 1893), 397. IX: VI (September 30, 1893), 429. X: VI (October 7, 1893), 461. XI: VI (October 14, 1893), 475–76. XII: VI (October 21, 1893), 508. XIII: VI (October 28, 1893), 558–60. XIV: VI (November 11, 1893), 606. XV: VI (November 18, 1893), 636. XVI: VI (November 25, 1893), 668. XVII: VI (December 2, 1893), 700. XVIII: VI (December 9, 1893), 732. XIX: VI (December 23, 1893), 796. XX: VI (December 30, 1893), 828. XXI: VII (January 6, 1894), 25–26. XXII: VII (January 13, 1894), 36. XXIII: VII (January 20, 1894), 70–71. XXIV: VII (January 27, 1894), 117–20.

"In the Change of Years," *Black and White*, VII (January 6, 1894), 18–22.

"Letters to [or from] a Débutante, I–VIII," *Punch*, CVI, CVII, and CVIII (May 26, 1894, to January 26, 1895). I: CVI (May 26, 1894), 251. II: CVI (June 16, 1894), 285. III, CVI (June 23, 1894), 298. IV: CVII (October 6, 1894), 168. V: CVII (October 13, 1894), 180. VI: CVII (October 27, 1894), 193. VII: CVII (November 17, 1894), 229. VIII: CVIII (January 26, 1895), 46.

"The Minx—A Poem in Prose," *Punch*, CVII (July 21, 1894), 33.

"A Phalse Note on George the Fourth," *Punch*, CVII (October 27, 1894), 204.

"A Few Words with Mr. Max Beerbohm," *Sketch*, VIII (January 2,

1895), 439. Reprinted in Violet Wyndham, *The Sphinx and Her Circle*. New York: Vanguard, 1964, pp. 45–48.

"Overheard Fragment of a Dialogue," *Punch*, CVIII (January 12, 1895), 24. Reprinted in Violet Wyndham, *The Sphinx and Her Circle*. New York: Vanguard, 1964, pp. 48–50.

"From the Queer and Yellow Book," I: 1894; II: "Tooraloora, A Fragment," *Punch*, CVIII (February 2, 1895), 58.

"The Advisability of Not Being Brought Up in a Handbag: A Trivial Tragedy for Wonderful People," *Punch*, CVIII (March 2, 1895), 107. Reprinted in Violet Wyndham, *The Sphinx and Her Circle*. New York: Vanguard, 1964, pp. 50–51.

"Suggestion," *Yellow Book*, V (April, 1895), 249–57.

"The Age of Love" (two letters to the Editor), *Punch*, CIX (September 21, 1895), 141.

"Letters to [or from] a Fiancée, I–IV," *Punch*, CIX (September 28, 1895, to November 2, 1895). I: CIX (September 28, 1895), 149. II: CIX (October 5, 1895), 159. III: CIX (October 12, 1895), 169. IV: CIX (November 2, 1895), 207.

"The Plain Tale of Cinderella, Told by Three Authors [No. I. By R-dy-rd K-pl-ng; No. II. By J-hn Ol-v-r H-bbs; No. III. By G--rge M--re]," *Punch*, CIX (November 30, 1895), 264.

" 'Be It Cosiness' [By Max Mereboom]," *Punch*, CIX (December 21, 1895), 297.

"The Quest of Sorrow," *Yellow Book*, VIII (January, 1896), 325–35.

"Letters of Marjorie and Gladys, I: The Decline of Flirtation," *Punch*, CXI (November 28, 1896), 253; ". . . II: About Astrology and Things of That Sort," *Punch*, CXI (December 12, 1896), 277.

"Sketches in London, I: In a Boudoir," *Punch*, CXIII (July 17, 1897), 16–17.

*The Triflers* (unfinished, unpublished play).

"White and Gold," *Referee*, June 28, 1903, to August 20, 1905, usually p. 7, sometimes p. 9. No column in issue of June 5, 1904. Total of 113 columns.

*The Twelfth Hour*. London: Grant Richards, 1907. Reprinted London: Chapman and Hall, 1951.

*Love's Shadow*. London: Grant Richards, 1908. Reprinted London: Chapman and Hall, 1950. Reprinted in *The Little Ottleys*. London: MacGibbon and Kee, 1962; New York: Norton, 1963.

*The Limit*. London: Grant Richards, 1911. Reprinted London: Chapman and Hall, 1950. Reprinted New York: Norton, 1951. Reprinted New York: Curtis Books, 1972.

*Tenterhooks*. London: Grant Richards, 1912. Reprinted London: Chapman and Hall, 1951. Reprinted in *The Little Ottleys*. London: MacGibbon and Kee, 1962; New York: Norton, 1963.

*Bird of Paradise*. London: Grant Richards, 1914. Reprinted London: Chapman and Hall, 1951. Reprinted New York: Norton, 1952.

"Introduction" to *Whom You Should Marry*, London: Grant Richards, 1915, pp. 5–9.

*Love at Second Sight*. London: Grant Richards, 1916. Reprinted London: Chapman and Hall, 1951. Reprinted in *The Little Ottleys*. London: MacGibbon and Kee, 1962; New York: Norton, 1963.

"Free Verse," *English Review*, XXIX (December, 1919), 534–36.

"The Blow," *English Review*, XXXI (December, 1920), 515–20. Also appeared in *Living Age*, CCCVIII (January 8, 1921), 111–14.

"Gentlemen *v*. Players: A Critic Match," *English Review*, XXXIV (April, 1922), 331–34.

"The Last First Night," *Criterion*, IV (January, 1926), 148–53. Reprinted in *Letters to the Sphinx*. London: Duckworth, 1930.

*Letters to the Sphinx from Oscar Wilde, with Reminiscences of the Author*. London: Duckworth, 1930.

*The Little Ottleys (Love's Shadow; Tenterhooks; Love at Second Sight)*. Introduction by Colin MacInnes. London: MacGibbon and Kee, 1962; New York: Norton, 1963.

## SECONDARY SOURCES

"Ada Leverson's Return." Review of *The Little Ottleys*, *Times Literary Supplement*, August 24, 1962, p. 637. Conservative notice; reviewer finds MacInnes, in his introduction to *The Little Ottleys*, exaggerates Mrs. Leverson's artistry. Despite her percipience and humor, she is careless and perfunctory both in style and in construction.

ALINGTON, ADRIAN. Review of *Love's Shadow* and *The Limit*, *Public Opinion*, December 8, 1950, pp. 18–19. In the nostalgic, period charm of her novels, Mrs. Leverson is superior to "Saki" because she can "strike deeper," and, especially in *The Limit*, she transcends the "tiny, frivolous, Edwardian coterie" to become "a writer of real distinction."

ANON. Review of *Love's Shadow*, *Academy*, LXXIV (June 20, 1908), 909–10. Representative contemporary review; highly praises the naturalness, restraint, truth-to-life of Mrs. Leverson, "an artist of rare quality."

ANON. Review of *The Limit*, *Standard*, March 17, 1911, p. 5. Typical contemporary review in a London newspaper; finds Leverson in spontaneity and originality closer to Lewis Carroll than to any other English humorist.

BERGONZI, BERNARD. "Woman of Some Importance." Review of *The Little Ottleys*, *Spectator*, CCIX (August 31, 1962), 311. Charges MacInnes heavily underestimated the indebtedness of Leverson to

Wilde. Singles out for special praise Mrs. Leverson's brilliant dialogue, her handling of sexual feeling "without a sense of heavy breathing and general embarrassment," and her "beautiful sense of comedy." Alert, sympathetic commentary.

BLIVEN, NAOMI. "It's Not a Woman's World." Review of *The Little Ottleys*, *New Yorker*, XXXIX (June 1, 1963), 111–14. With an earlier article in the *New Yorker* by Anthony West, the most negative criticism of Mrs. Leverson's novels ever written. Mrs. Leverson's novels are terrible—"terrible in an engaging, funny, pitiable way—not art but artlessness, the daydreams of their author."

BROWN, JOHN MASON. "Edwardian Sphinx." Review of *The Limit*, *Saturday Review*, XXXIV (September 1, 1951), 21–22. Reprinted in *As They Appear* (New York: McGraw Hill, 1952), pp. 11–17. Good, short general introduction to Mrs. Leverson; many details derived from Sitwell's *Noble Essences*. Sees Leverson's spirit and tone in her comedy as more like Wilde, particularly in *The Importance of Being Earnest*, than any other contemporary.

BURKHART, CHARLES. "Ada Leverson and Oscar Wilde," *English Literature in Transition*, XIII, no. 3 (1970), 193–200. Influence of Oscar Wilde, both personal and literary, on Mrs. Leverson and her writing.

"The Edwardians." Review of *Tenterhooks* and *Love at Second Sight*, *Times Literary Supplement*, March 23, 1951, p. 177. Though witty and often extraordinarily vivid in their portrait of pre-World War I England, *Tenterhooks* and, especially, *Love at Second Sight*, have faulty construction; lack objectivity in the presentation of their paragon heroine, Edith Ottley.

HOLDEN, INEZ. "The Art of Ada Leverson," *Cornhill Magazine*, CLXIV (Summer, 1950), 429–38. Considers Leverson's two greatest qualities to be readability and lightness of touch. *The Limit*, "probably her best novel," is analyzed extensively. Mrs. Leverson has in common with Firbank, Maurice Baring, and Saki "sudden inconsequences, a kind of occasional near-silliness in style, which seems to distinguish the writer of a leisured class, and comes perhaps from social confidence."

LEWIS, D. B. WYNDHAM. "Edwardian Afternoons." Review of *Love's Shadow* and *The Limit*, *Tablet*, CXCVI (December 9, 1950), 513. Finds the novels, for all their kindliness and gaiety, most interesting as a picture of a charming but dead way of life; Mrs. Leverson's world was "that top-hatted Pompeii on the eve of the cataclysm."

MACINNES, COLIN. "The Heart of a Legend," *Encounter*, XVI (May, 1961), 46–65. Reprinted in *England, Half English* (London: MacGibbon and Kee, 1961), pp. 158–82. Also reprinted as the introduction to *The Little Ottleys* (London: MacGibbon and Kee, 1962; New York: Norton, 1963). Mrs. Leverson's status as "a very great artist indeed" has been obscured in various ways: the legend of Wilde—a lesser writer—has engulfed her; Osbert Sitwell's memoir of her in *Noble Essences* focused on her as a character rather than as a writer; she herself was unconcerned over her literary reputation; she has been regarded as a period writer and only as that. However, her detachment from the Edwardian scene she so closely observed makes her essentially modern. Her type of comedy of manners is the same as Congreve's. The extent to which Mr. MacInnes' claims for Mrs. Leverson's artistry are exaggerated is shown by the lack of evidence for the formal ability he attributes to her; but the enthusiasm of his overstated yet extremely well-written essay, together with his account of her chief themes of marriage and friendship and with his selection of moments of high comedy from the six novels, makes it one of the best Leverson critiques.

MITCHELL, JULIAN. Review of *The Little Ottleys, London Magazine*, n.s. II (December, 1962), 80–81. Leverson's novels still deserve to be read because she is "an admirably serious and genuinely witty writer." "Resignation, acceptance of one's role in other people's lives, is a main theme of the novels. . . ." World War I ended her novel-writing career because it was "too big a subject for comedy, even comedy of her seriousness. . . ."

MORTIMER, RAYMOND. "The Edwardians." Review of *Love's Shadow* and *The Limit, Sunday Times*, November 12, 1950, p. 3. The republication of Mrs. Leverson's novels may mark the beginning of a revival of interest in the Edwardian period, that "shamelessly money-minded" but elegant era. Although in her novels the "wit shimmers rather than dazzles," the characters are types not individuals; "the plots would be almost substantial enough to make short stories"; the charm of her novels lies in their "absurd insubstantiality."

PRITCHETT, V. S. "The Knightsbridge Kennels." Review of *The Little Ottleys, New Statesman*, LXIV (August 31, 1962), 257–58. Reprinted in *The Living Novel and Later Appreciations* (New York: Random House, 1964), pp. 263–69. One of the two or three best critical studies of Mrs. Leverson. Particularly good on characterization; on the limitations inherent in minor comedies of manners; on the theme of integrity in the novels.

QUENNELL, PETER. "Sphinx stands up to the test of time." Review of *Love's Shadow* and *The Limit, Daily Mail*, November 18, 1950, p. 2. Also appeared in *Continental Daily Mail*, same date. Leverson's novels are "relics of that selfish, sunshiny age preceding the

Grand Deluge", attractive enough in their economy, wit, and tenderness that long-winded and sententious modern novelists could learn from them.

RICHARDS, GRANT. *Memories of a Misspent Youth.* London: Heinemann, 1932, pp. 300–301. Importance of the Sphinx in the 1890's; Richards' efforts—finally successful—to persuade her to write a novel; one or two Sphinx witticisms.

SCANNELL, VERNON. Review of *The Little Ottleys, Listener*, LXVIII (September 6, 1962), 365. Leverson's lightness, delicacy, and elegance enable her to say a great deal more about "honour, love, duty, and the absurdities and glories of passion" than far more portentous writers.

SITWELL, SIR OSBERT. "Ada Leverson," in *Noble Essences.* Boston: Little, Brown, 1950. A shorter version appeared as "Ada Leverson, Wilde & 'Max,'" *National and English Review*, CXXXV (September, 1950), 286–90. Sir Osbert's very personal memoir of the Sphinx is the authority which dozens of later writers have used. He pictures her in her later years; especially vivid in his description of her sojourns in Italy; but includes many details of earlier days. Little or no comment on the Sphinx's writing; but probably the fullest account of the Sphinx as a wit. A little patronizing and sometimes inaccurate; nonetheless, an excellent source.

———. "Obituary," *Times*, September 1, 1933, p. 17. Mrs. Leverson's capacity for living in the present, her gentleness, her acuteness as literary critic, and her association with Wilde are recalled in Sir Osbert's obituary notice.

SMITH, STEVIE. "The Wittiest Woman in the World." Review of *Love's Shadow* and *The Limit, Britain Today*, April, 1951, n.p. Much of the interest of Leverson's novels is their evocation of the Edwardian period. Mrs. Leverson establishes her characters through dialogue "with great skill."

SNOW, C. P. Review of *Love's Shadow* and *The Limit, Spectator*, CLXXXVI (January 19, 1951), 82. Compares Mrs. Leverson with Firbank; prefers Mrs. Leverson's more traditional approach to human experience to Firbank's "moment-by-moment technique."

STONIER, G. W. Review of *Love's Shadow* and *The Limit;* and of *The Twelfth Hour* and *Bird of Paradise, New Statesman,* n.s. XLIII (January 5, 1952), 16–17. Leverson's novels worth reviving because they are good, light comedies of manners that mirror a way of life that died with World War I.

STRONG, L. A. G. "Edwardian Summers." Review of *Tenterhooks* and *Love at Second Sight, Public Opinion,* June 15, 1951, p. 21. Fairly negative, though Mrs. Leverson's novels, because of "many small felicities" and their "bouquet of those foundered Edwardian summers," are "well worth exhuming." Mrs. Leverson's famous wit is not much in evidence in these novels, and her construction is poor —*Tenterhooks* is "hardly more than a charade" and *Love at Second Sight* is only "a series of episodes"; principal fault is lack of self-discipline which shows mainly in her lack of objectivity about her characters.

"Visiting the Sphinx." Review of *Love's Shadow* and *The Limit, Times Literary Supplement,* December 29, 1950, p. 825. Lack of form keeps her novels from the first rank, but her wit is second to none among her contemporaries. Her atmosphere is more convincing than Saki's. "Ada Leverson was wedded to an outward cynicism that protects much romantic feeling."

WEST, ANTHONY. "Out of the Dead Past." Review of *The Limit, New Yorker*, XXVII (August 18, 1951), 82–84. Harshest criticism of a novel by Mrs. Leverson ever written. Contrived, unfunny, and shallow, *The Limit* is worth reading only to learn how much novelists have improved in their craft since its era.

WYNDHAM, VIOLET. *The Sphinx and Her Circle: A Memoir of Ada Leverson by Her Daughter*. London: André Deutsch, 1963; New York: Vanguard, 1964. Chapters II and III were published in slightly different form as "Ada Leverson" in *Cornhill*, CLXXIII (Spring, 1963), 147–63. The most important work on Ada Leverson. Mrs. Wyndham's book is a vivid and candid account of her mother's life, career, friends, and personality. Especially valuable for its picture of London in the 1890's, of the Edwardian era, and for real-life prototypes of the characters in the novels. Many memorable examples of the wit of the Sphinx, of Wilde, and of others. Some of Mrs. Leverson's shorter pieces are quoted in full.

# Index